Champion of Truth
The Life of Saint Athanasius

MICHAEL E. MOLLOY

ST PAULS

Alba
House

Library of Congress Cataloging-in-Publication Data

Molloy, Michael E.
  Champion of truth : the life of Saint Athanasius / Michael E. Molloy.
    p. cm.
  Includes bibliographical references.
    ISBN 0-8189-0945-5
  1. Athanasius, Saint, Patriarch of Alexandria, d. 373. 2. Christian
saints—Egypt—Biography. I. Title.

BR1720.A7 .M65 2003
270.2'092—dc21

                                    2002151883

Produced and designed in the United States of America by the
Fathers and Brothers of the Society of St. Paul,
2187 Victory Boulevard, Staten Island, New York 10314,
as part of their communications apostolate.

ISBN 0-8189-0945-5

Printing Information:

Current Printing - first digit 1 2 3 4 5 6 7 8 9 10

Year of Current Printing - first year shown

2003 2004 2005 2006 2007 2008 2009 2010 2011 2012

To my wife Rita

CONTENTS

Preface xv

Introduction xvii

Chapter 1: Early Years 1

Chapter 2: The Arians 13

Chapter 3: The Council of Nicea 21

Chapter 4: The New Bishop 29

Chapter 5: Intrigue 37

Chapter 6: Exile 47

Chapter 7: Pastor and Teacher 63

Chapter 8: The Desert 71

Chapter 9: The Last Years 81

Appendix A: Alexandria 93

Appendix B: Life in Egypt 101

Appendix C: The Church in Egypt 109

Appendix D: Constantine 113

Appendix E: Monasticism 119

Appendix F: A Guide for the Use of the Psalms 123

Appendix G: The Importance of Chanting the Psalms 127

Notes 129

Bibliography 133

CHRONOLOGY

298 A.D.	Birth of Athanasius
303	Diocletian persecution begins
311	Bishop Peter of Alexandria martyred
312	Conversion of Constantine
313	Constantine ends persecution
318	*On the Incarnation* written
319	Arian controversy begins
323	Constantine sole Emperor
325	Council of Nicea
328	Death of Alexander
	Athanasius consecrated Bishop
329	Visit to Thebaid
331	Athanasius' defense before Constantine
335	Council of Tyre
	First exile begins (in Gaul)
336	Death of Arius
337	Death of Constantine
	Constantius, Constans, and Constantine II co-Caesars
	Athanasius returns to Egypt
338	Antony visits Alexandria
339	Second exile begins (in Italy)
346	Athanasius returns to Egypt
350	Constans murdered
	Constantius sole Emperor
351?	*Defense Against the Arians* written
356	Third exile begins (in the desert)
	Life of Antony written
358	*History of the Arians* written

361   Death of Constantius
        Julian Emperor
362   Athanasius returns from exile
        Fourth exile begins (in the desert)
363   Death of Julian
        Jovian Emperor
364   Athanasius returns from exile
        Death of Jovian
        Valentinian and Valens co-Caesars
365   Fifth exile begins (at country house)
366   Athanasius returns from exile
370   Memorial Church dedicated
373   Death of Athanasius

ON THE GREAT ATHANASIUS

by Saint Gregory Nazianzen

To speak of and admire him fully, would perhaps be too long a task…. He was noble in action, humble in mind, unapproachable in virtue, very approachable in conversation, gentle, free from anger, sympathetic, sweet in words, sweeter in disposition; angelic in appearance, more angelic in mind, calm in rebuke, persuasive in praise…. His disposition sufficed for the training of his spiritual children with very little need for words…. His life and habits form the ideal of a bishop and his teaching the law of orthodoxy….

[To the monks] … whatever he thought was for them a law, whatever on the contrary he disapproved, they renounced. His decisions were to them the tables of Moses, and they paid more reverence [to him] than is due to the Saints….

Let one praise him in his fastings and prayers as if he had been without a body and immaterial, another his tirelessness and zeal for vigils and psalmody, another his support of the needy, another his unyielding stance towards the powerful, or his condescension to the lowly. Let the virgins celebrate the friend of the Bridegroom… hermits [the one] who gives wings to their course, cenobites their lawgiver, simple folk their guide, contemplatives their theologian… the unfortunate their consolation, the elderly their staff, youths their instructor, the poor their resource, the wealthy their steward. Even the widows will, I think, praise their

protector, even the orphans their father, even the poor their bene-
factor, strangers their host, brothers the man of brotherly love, the
sick their physician....

In a good old age he ended his life, and was gathered to his
fathers, the Patriarchs, and Prophets, and Apostles, and Martyrs,
who contended for the faith.

Excerpted from the oration *On the Great Athanasius* in the *Nicene and Post-Nicene Fathers, Vol. VII: Gregory Nazianzen*, edited by P. Schaff (Eerdmans Publ. Co., Grand Rapids, reprinted 1975).

APOSTICHA OF VESPERS
FOR SAINT ATHANASIUS

Hail, O model of virtue, who fought valiantly for the faith and shattered the heresy of Arius by the power of your sacred words, O Athanasius, as you clearly taught of the one power shared by the three Persons of the Holy Trinity. By it, all things spiritual and material have been created in its unique goodness. Thus you explained that which is difficult to understand in the divine creation. Beg Christ to send great mercy to our souls.

Hail, O support of patriarchs, clear trumpet, sublime spirit, precise tongue, penetrating insight, radiance of just doctrine, true shepherd and resplendent torch, axe chopping down the weeds of heresy to burn them in the fire of the Spirit, unshakable pillar, unassailable citadel: you preached the supreme power of the Holy Trinity. Intercede before God to send great mercy to our souls!

Hail, O star shining resplendently over the whole world through the exploits of your struggles, eclipsing the glory of Arius into a sad twilight, O heavenly spirit, filled with renown, who made your brilliant teachings radiate over all of us orthodox, teaching that the Son shares with the Father the same nature, throne, and honor. Ceaselessly beg the divine Spirit, consubstantial and indivisible, to send great mercy to our souls.

From the *January Menaion* (Sophia Press, Newton Centre, 1992). Reprinted with permission.

PREFACE

It has been nearly three decades since I first learned of the inspiring, fourth-century bishop from Egypt named Athanasius. My introduction to him came through a correspondence course offered by Saint Athanasius Academy of Orthodox Theology in Goleta, California. At that time Fr. Jack Sparks, Fr. Jon Braun, and Fr. Richard Ballew were instructors at the Academy. The life of Athanasius had such a profound effect upon them that they named both their academy and their local church after him. It was through a course taught by Fr. Richard Ballew on fourth-century Christology that I encountered "Athanasius the Great." He has been a hero of mine ever since.

Over the ensuing years it has always been my hope that more people could have the opportunity to learn about this wonderful saint. Unfortunately, there has not been a biography of his life available that was geared for the general reader. (This has been due in part to the simple lack of information about his personal life.) On a visit to Alaska a few years ago Bishop Kallistos of England mentioned that the best source still available on his life was the introduction to Athanasius' writings in the fourth volume of the *Nicene and Post-Nicene Fathers* series. I was glad that I had a copy, but I also knew that this is a book which the general reader would probably never even pick up. (Its translation is outdated and its format is difficult to follow.) I felt that someone needed to write a popular version of his life. In time, I decided to make an attempt myself. This book is the result of that effort.

I do not claim anything original in this biography, except for the errors. I have simply tried to follow those who came before me. In this regard, I am indebted most to Fr. Richard Ballew for his study of Athanasius and the Arian controversy. It is important to acknowledge the help that others gave me during the writing of this book. Robin Armstrong offered suggestions on the final draft. Mary Alice Cook proofread the text. Fr. Marc Dunaway gave me his encouragement along the way. My wife Rita, and our children, Stephen and Regina, were very gracious for allowing me to spend so many hours on this project. In addition, I cannot fail to mention Fr. Harold and Barbara Dunaway, who have been such wonderful examples of Christian love and leadership.

Throughout most of my adult life Saint Athanasius has been a continual source of inspiration to me. His courageous and life-long battle for the truth saved the Church from disaster. Because of this, every Christian, whether he knows it or not, owes him a debt of gratitude. This biography is in part meant to fulfill my own debt to him. If Athanasius becomes a hero to any of my readers, this book will have fulfilled its purpose.

Fr. Michael E. Molloy
January 18, 2003
Saint Athanasius

(A note to the reader: those who desire more historical background on the life of Athanasius may choose to read the appendices first.)

INTRODUCTION

Saint Athanasius was one of the great leaders of the early Church. During the fourth century there were many great men and women of faith, but none of them did more to further the cause of Christ than this diminutive bishop from Egypt. Trying times require the best of men and the best from men, and that is exactly what the Church got in Athanasius. At a time when the Church faced the most insidious heresy of all, one man rose above all others to combat it — and combat it he did. On several occasions his great struggle for the truth brought him near to martyrdom. But instant martyrdom was not to be God's will for his life. Instead, he was to spend the fifty years of his adult life in a courageous, bloodless, martyrdom, tenaciously fighting for the true Christian faith.

For the last seventeen centuries every generation of Christians has given Athanasius praise. To all who confess the deity of Christ, he is a shining example. Athanasius was as true a champion of the truth as ever lived. He stood tall for the faith when others withered. He did not flinch even from the threats of emperors. For a time it seemed that he was battling alone against the whole world (thus the famous Latin phrase: "Athanasius contra mundum"). His life was the stuff of legend. His experiences were sometimes stranger than fiction. But to the praise and glory of God, he was very real indeed. To those who know about his life, even the very mention of his name stirs the soul.

Athanasius was the Patriarchal Bishop of the Church of

Alexandria and of all Egypt. In this office he served for four and a half decades. As a youth he endured the greatest persecution that the Church had ever seen. As a bishop he fought against the greatest heresy of all time. Throughout all these years, Athanasius remained an indefatigable soldier of God. Though short of stature, his wonderful life and great deeds have cast a very long shadow.

Saint Athanasius was born in the year 298 A.D. in Alexandria, Egypt. From infancy he was raised by devout parents in the ways of the Christian faith. When he was only five years old, the great persecution under Diocletian began. It lasted for ten years. What would have been the normal years of his youth were swallowed up in the struggle for survival. Terrible things happened. Churches were desecrated and destroyed. Christians were brutally persecuted. The faithful were imprisoned, tortured, and killed in horrible ways. No persecution before had ever been so widespread or so systematic. In the year 313 the persecution finally came to an end when Constantine the Great became the first Christian Emperor. Christians then went from being persecuted by the government to being favored by the government. During that same year Alexander was consecrated as the new Patriarch of Alexandria. The teenage Athanasius soon came to his notice. The Bishop was impressed with the young man and decided to personally take him under his wing. Alexander guided his formal education and also served as his mentor in the things of the Church. Athanasius grew in wisdom and knowledge, and in due time he was ordained to the diaconate. Following his ordination, Alexander appointed him to be his personal archdeacon.

For awhile the Church enjoyed a much needed peace, but this peace was not to last. A new scourge soon came upon the faithful. This time the attack came not from outside the Church, but from within. The new scourge was a heresy called Arianism. It was started by a priest of Alexandria named Arius, who promoted a theology that departed from the ancient faith of the Church. He taught that Christ was not the divine and eternal Son of God the Father, but merely a created being. Those who embraced his heresy were called Arians. Their byword became: "there was a time when he was not." In other words, they believed that there was a time when the Word and Son of God did not exist.

Though Arianism was condemned by Patriarch Alexander and the bishops of Egypt, it continued to grow and spread. Eventually, the first Ecumenical Council of the Church was called to deal with it. In the year 325 over three hundred bishops, along with many other clergy, gathered at Nicea in Asia Minor. Though only a deacon at the time, Athanasius played an important role in the proceedings. At the Council the bishops pronounced Arianism to be a heresy and they reaffirmed the true faith of the Apostles. This affirmation was summarized by the Council in the famous statement of faith known as the Nicene Creed. In addition, Arius and his followers were condemned. However, this was not to be the end of the Arians.

In the year 328 Bishop Alexander died and Athanasius was chosen as his successor. As the new Patriarch of Alexandria and Egypt, he worked zealously for the good of the Church. He became the staunchest defender of the truth that had been proclaimed at Nicea. The Arians understood fully that the Patriarch was their principal foe, and they worked feverishly against him. In time, through intrigue, lies, conspiracy, and threats, they gained a following with hierarchs and civil authorities in the East. Eventually, they even persuaded the Emperor Constantine to send Athanasius off to exile in Gaul in the year 335. This exile was to be the first of many. In the decades to come, he would be exiled on five separate occasions for a total of seventeen years. The Patriarch spent the rest of his life fighting against the Arians. In the end, thanks to God, the theology of Nicea prevailed. For his lifelong defense of the truth, Athanasius is called the "Father of Orthodoxy."

During his lifetime Athanasius wrote several books. His work *On the Incarnation* is one of the best ever written on the subject. He was just nineteen years old when he wrote it. Many of his works were penned to counter the Arian heresy. These included the *History of the Arians* and the *Defense Against the Arians*. The most famous of his writings during his lifetime was the *Life of Antony*. His biography of Saint Antony, the great desert ascetic, was a "best seller" of the day. This book did much to promote the cause of monasticism. Indeed, Athanasius always had a special place in his heart for the monastics, and they for him.

Athanasius' entire life was one of complete dedication to God. He strove mightily for the faith and never wavered in the cause for truth. His life and deeds remain as an example of self-sacrifice and loyalty to God. Through his efforts, Arianism was overcome and the true Christian faith was preserved. For this every Christian owes him a debt of gratitude. Athanasius was one of the greatest fathers of the early Church. His legacy, like a beacon, has continued to shine throughout the ages.

CHAMPION OF TRUTH

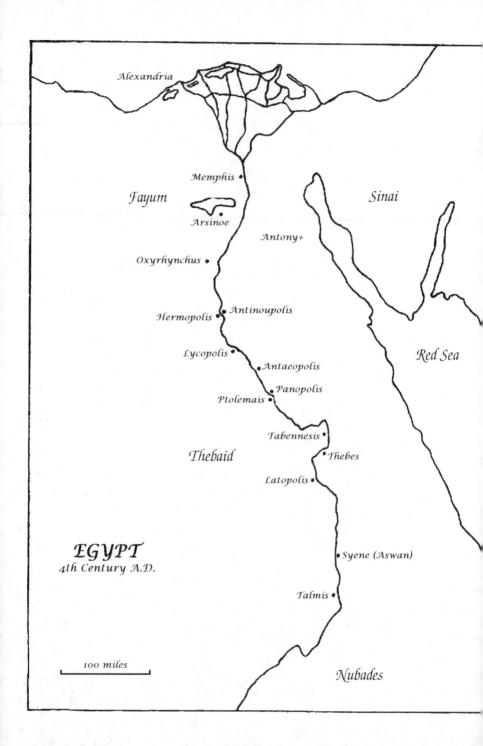

Alexandria

Fayum

Memphis •

Arsinoe

Oxyrhynchus •

Hermopolis • • Antinoupolis

Lycopolis •

• Antaeopolis

• Panopolis

Ptolemais •

• Tabennesis

Thebaid

• Thebes

Latopolis •

Sinai

Antony+

Red Sea

EGYPT
4th Century A.D.

• Syene (Aswan)

Talmis •

100 miles

Nubades

CHAPTER ONE

EARLY YEARS

"Train a child in the way he should go,
and when he is old he will not depart from it."
Proverbs 22:6

Saint Athanasius was born in a tumultuous age. At the time of
his birth, the city of Alexandria and all of Egypt were in great
turmoil. For three centuries the Egyptians had endured Roman
rule. Since the days of Julius Caesar and Cleopatra the nation had
lived under this foreign occupation. It was a bitter pill to swallow
for a people who had known such greatness. For millennia the land
of the Pharaohs had been the greatest civilization on earth, but
that power was no more. Egypt was now the bread basket of Rome.
The grain from the fertile Nile valley was shipped to feed the con-
querors. It was impossible for discontent not to smolder. The sight
of the great Pyramids was a constant reminder of the greatness
that was no more. Resentment had built up to the boiling point.
The revolutionary leader Lucius Domitius Domitianus caused it
to boil over.

In the year 297 Lucius organized a rebel army to overthrow
the Romans. His zeal was more than patriotic. He wanted to rule
himself. He was a very wealthy man and had the means to finance

the rebels. The Roman garrisons were unprepared for the sudden uprising and within weeks Lucius' forces had gained control of much of Egypt. The news of this rebellion made its way quickly to the Emperor Diocletian. The situation was serious. Not only was the rule of Egypt at stake, but also the bread of Rome. Diocletian took the matter so seriously that he did not just send his best generals to Egypt — he came himself. He was determined to crush the rebellion.

When the Emperor arrived in Egypt in October, he found the great city of Alexandria well fortified. He decided to let it be — for the moment. Leaving troops to guard the city entrances so that no one might enter or leave, he marched on. He had with him five legions of Rome's best soldiers. Egypt was no match for them. One by one, as dominoes toppling in a row, each city, town, and village fell before the mighty Roman army. The rebels were quickly decimated. By December only Alexandria was left to conquer. But before Diocletian attacked the city he sent his envoys with a message: if the city would surrender, the people would be spared (no doubt with the exception of Lucius and his leaders). From atop the city walls the answer came back. The profanity and insults cannot be repeated, but the basic answer was a contemptuous "No!"

When the Emperor learned of the reply, he was not just angry, he was infuriated. He made an oath and vowed that when the city was taken, and taken it would be, the slaughter of life would not stop until the blood reached his horse's knees. This vow was to prove fateful for the city. The attack was prepared in the spring of 298. The feared Roman machines of war were brought into place. Troops were gathered. Arms were readied. And then it began. The catapults launched projectiles into and over the walls. The massive battering ram beat against the city gates. Arrows flew.

It was only a matter of time. Finally, the gates were breached and the army poured into Alexandria like a flood — a flood of death, maiming, butchery, and blood. For two days it continued. Then Diocletian rode in to observe the carnage, and as he did, his horse slipped on the bloodied pavement and fell. Its knees were bloodied. Whether the Emperor felt bound to keep his oath, or had simply tired of the slaughter, is only conjecture, but he halted the siege. The city had been taken. The killing was stopped. The conquered citizens, relieved by the end of the bloodshed, later erected a statue — in honor of the Emperor's horse.

During this time of great upheaval Athanasius' mother was pregnant with him. Sometime during the siege of the city or shortly thereafter she gave birth. Athanasius came into the world in the midst of turmoil. And this beginning was to make a mark upon his life. In turmoil he was born and in turmoil he would live.

Athanasius was born into a devout Christian family. As was the custom, he was baptized and chrismated while still an infant. While just a "babe in arms" he accompanied his parents to the services of the Church. And as everyone there prayed and worshipped, so he prayed and worshipped, too — as babies do. Before he was old enough to walk, the life of faith and worship were familiar to him: the music of the Psalter, the chiming of the bells, the fragrance of the incense, the glimmer of the candles, the chanting of the prayers, the sprinkling of the holy water, the gaze of the icons, the taste of the Eucharist.

As he grew older, his parents taught him the essentials: faith, hope, and love. They told him the stories of the Old Testament: Adam and Eve, Noah and the great Flood, Abraham and Lot, Moses and the Red Sea, David and Goliath, Elijah and the fiery chariot, Job and his patience, Daniel and the lion's den, the three holy youths and the fiery furnace, Jonah and the whale. They explained to him the Ten Commandments. They told him of John the Baptist and the coming of the Messiah, Jesus Christ the Lord. He learned the great stories of Jesus' life including his crucifixion, death, burial, resurrection, and ascension. The psalms of praise and the prayers of the hours were second nature to him. By the age of five he had received a strong foundation in the faith. He would need it. The next lesson that would come was nothing less than the unleashing of Hell on earth.

In the year 303 the greatest persecution that the Church had ever seen swept over Egypt. It had begun with the encouragement of Galerius, who was co-regent in the East. He convinced the Emperor Diocletian that the Christians were an offense to the gods of Rome. Since they worshipped only the Christian God and not the traditional deities, they brought dishonor to the Empire. Their disrespect for the gods was also disrespect for the emperor himself. In short, they were guilty of treason.

Diocletian believed that his success as a leader had come because of favor that he had received from the gods. To continue in their favor, he desired that everyone pay homage to them. He agreed with Galerius that harsh measures were warranted in order to accomplish this. Naively, he believed that Christians could be forced to worship the gods of Rome. He did not understand, however, that for a Christian this act would be an abomination. To worship the gods, would be to deny the One True God. This no faithful Christian would do.

The Emperor then issued the first edict of the persecution. It called for the destruction of churches. The holy books were to be surrendered and burned. Sacred vessels were to be confiscated. Christians who refused to offer sacrifice to the gods lost their legal rights, forfeited any offices or titles held, and could be tortured. In the weeks that followed the issuance of the edict, however, few were forced to sacrifice. Some churches were demolished. Some clergy were imprisoned. Many were flogged.

The persecution intensified when Maximin, the governor of Egypt, began to zealously carry out the edict. No one could identify all the Christians, but the clergy were readily known. They became the chief targets. Maximin ordered his officials to pressure the clergy into sacrificing. Not every official had the stomach for this. Some implored their prisoners to just make the gesture, to drop the incense on the charcoal and to comply with the law. Some gave in and did. Most refused and were sent to prison. Some were sent off to the mines to undergo forced labor. Others were tortured to death.

A few weeks after the first edict, two fires broke out in the imperial palace in Nicomedia. Christians were conveniently blamed for starting the fires. As a result, new edicts followed. Persecution intensified. Now torture and execution were to be used without hesitation. "Burn the godless at the stake" was Diocletian's sentiment. All clergy were to be imprisoned unless they surrendered the holy books and sacred vessels, and sacrificed to the gods. Some did. Most remained faithful.

The filthy dungeons, which were built to house murderers and thieves, now contained bishops, priests, and deacons. So many of them were arrested that the prisons were filled to overflowing, and more prisoners were added daily. Officials complained that there was no longer any room for criminals, and that robbers and murderers roamed free. Their townspeople felt that the streets were no longer safe and they feared for their families. Conditions in the prisons were abominable. There was barely even enough room for a man to sit, let alone lie down. Rats bit the prisoners and ate their food. The stench from human waste was terrible.

In the year 304 another edict was added to the misery. Christianity was made illegal and punishable by death. This edict provided the government with a solution to the overcrowding. Everyone who would not sacrifice to the gods would be tortured to death. The spectacle of what took place after this surpasses description. All regard for humanity was shackled and every evil was unleashed. Tortures so terrible were devised that they could only have come from one source, and it was not from men. It was as if the persecutors were engaged in some kind of inhuman contest to invent the most cruel tortures. Those arrested received various and horrible punishments. They were scourged, burned, drowned, crucified, impaled, ripped apart, mutilated, blinded, maimed, and beheaded. Indeed, at times so many were beheaded at once that the executioner's axe broke in pieces and out of fatigue the executioners had to relieve one another in turns. Most faced death with great courage and unshakable faith. Many were filled with joy for being counted worthy to suffer for Christ. They even sang songs of praise until their last breath.

Countless numbers suffered for the faith. Most of these were of the clergy. But many of the laity, both men and women, were killed as well. Even children were not spared. Some of the faithful had come forth voluntarily to seek martyrdom. Most had been spied out by the authorities. The great majority of Christians, however, were neither tortured, nor killed, since the government simply did not know who they all were. Instead, they suffered in silence. Their churches were destroyed. Their leaders were imprisoned, exiled, or killed. Their gatherings were prohibited. To survive they had to worship in secret. The Church became once again the "Church of the catacombs." There was always the ever-present danger that one might be called upon at any moment to die for the faith. Everyone suffered in their own way. Some were martyred in an instant, others languished in the prisons or in the mines, most suffered in secret. A wise man may distinguish among them.

All this took place during Athanasius' childhood — ten years of it. From age five to age fifteen he endured evils that no child should ever endure, saw horrors that no child should ever see, and heard terrors no child should ever hear. All that was holy to him was crushed — crushed beneath the tyranny of an Empire gone mad. Persecution had swept over Egypt like a great flood, and no Christian was immune to it. Athanasius knew clergy, friends, relatives, and even playmates who had been arrested, imprisoned, tortured, exiled, and murdered. He saw the churches destroyed, the faith scorned, the godly trampled. The persecution greatly affected his childhood. It became a crucible of fire for him. And in that fire his soul was purified like gold. While still a youth he gained the qualities of faithfulness, endurance, zeal, and courage that would carry him throughout the rest of his life. His character was shaped for the good in spite of the bad. God had tested Athanasius and had not found him wanting.

The persecution almost ended in 311. Galerius, who had encouraged the persecution to begin with, was struck with cancer of the bowels. He suffered horribly and became convinced that his disease was a punishment for having persecuted the Christians. On his deathbed he issued an edict of toleration which halted the persecution and allowed the Church to publicly meet once again. He even asked the Church to pray for him!

Peace was not to be, however. The ruler Maximin renewed the persecution in Egypt and Syria. Once again the Christians there came under attack. During this period of time, Peter, the Patriarch of Alexandria, was martyred. The persecution raged on for two more years.

Then in the year 312 an event occurred which would signal

the beginning of the end of this reign of terror. It took place at the Milvian Bridge near Rome. Constantine, the Caesar of the West in the regions of Britain and Gaul, had marched on Rome. Like his father before him, he had favored the Christians in Britain and Gaul and lessened the persecution there. His goal was to defeat Maxentius, the pagan ruler of Rome, and to unify the empire. As his legions prepared for battle, Constantine saw a vision in the sky in broad daylight. It was the sign of the Cross, along with the words "by this sign conquer." That night in a dream he was instructed to prepare the labarum as a standard for his troops. It was a banner monogrammed with the first two Greek letters of the word "Christ." These letters were also to be traced on the shields of his troops. Constantine obeyed what he took to be a divine command. The next day his army, fighting under the banner of Christ, defeated Maxentius and his forces. Constantine had won. He now took control of Rome, as did his ally Licinius in the East. The ruler Maximin was then forced to end the persecution of the Church in Egypt in the year 313.

Through his vision Constantine had experienced a conversion to Christ (or, at the least, whatever measure of faith he might have held before had become crystallized). After three centuries the Church now had its first Christian Emperor. Changes came quickly. Christianity went from being an illegal sect to the favored religion. Prisoners were released. Exiles were recalled. The clergy were given special status. Confiscated items were returned. Public monies were used to rebuild damaged churches. Sunday was made a public holiday. Innumerable services of thanksgiving were held throughout the realm. As a result, Christian joy reigned.

As the Church returned to normalcy, Alexander was chosen to be the new Patriarch of Alexandria. Shortly after his consecration, Athanasius caught his attention. Though still just a lad of fifteen, Athanasius already possessed Christian virtues well beyond his years. His devout way of life and serious demeanor, along with his deep faith and considerable knowledge, portended a future role in Church leadership. From the moment that the two met, a personal bond was formed. Athanasius soon came under the personal tutelage of Alexander.

Athanasius received his formal education at the School of Alexandria, the same school where many great men before him had learned, such as Clement and Origen, along with many others. His first love was theology, but as was the custom he also received instruction in philosophy and the Greek classics. He was an excellent student.

His most precious learning, however, did not come from the School. It came from the Bishop. His close association with the hierarch was invaluable. Alexander treated him like a son and closely watched over his advancement. The young man spent many hours in the company of the Bishop and his fellow clergy. He rubbed elbows with them. He listened to their conversations. He observed their manner of life. He soaked in their wisdom. He learned as much from their piety and humility as he did from their words. Things which can only be received from personal discipleship became his. Thus, he grew in wisdom and stature before God and men.

Proof of his youthful wisdom is seen by his early authorship. While just nineteen years of age he wrote two short books, which were actually two lengthy letters. These letters were written in response to a request for instruction from a friend named Macarius. The first of these books, entitled *Against the Gentiles*, was an apology for the Christian faith and a refutation of paganism. The second, and more well-known, was the book *On the Incarnation*. The latter is recognized by many as a masterpiece. It remains as one of the clearest and most concise works ever written on the doctrine of the Incarnation. It reveals a profound understanding of this important truth of our faith, an understanding which is even more remarkable considering the young age at which Athanasius wrote it. This understanding was summarized in the famous dictum: "God became man, that man might become god." The act of the Incarnation, of the Son of God becoming man, makes it possible for man to become deified, to share in the very life of God. This is none other than the fulfillment of Christ's command: "Therefore you are to be perfect, just as your Father in heaven is perfect." (Mt 5:48)

It was the sorry state of man, wrote Athanasius, that caused the Word to take on human form and to appear on earth. He was both born and manifested in a human body for our salvation. Though God the Son took on a human body, he was in no way limited by it. "The Word was not hedged in by His body, nor did His presence in the body prevent His being present elsewhere as well. When He moved His body He did not cease also to direct the universe by His Mind and might. No. The marvelous truth is, that being the Word, so far from being Himself contained by anything, He actually contained all things Himself. In creation He is present everywhere, yet is distinct in being from it; ordering, directing, giving life to all, containing all, yet is He Himself the Uncontained, existing solely in His Father... Existing in a human body, to which He Himself gives life, He is still Source of life to all the universe, present in every part of it, yet outside of the whole."[1]

During his youth, Athanasius also spent time with the great Saint Antony in the desert. When is uncertain, but it seems possible that his parents might have sent him into the desert for a period of time during the great persecution. Athanasius said that he had "poured water" over Antony's hands (a mark of discipleship which Elisha had done for Elijah the prophet in the Old Testament). This meant that he had been of personal service to Antony during his time there. How long Athanasius spent with the great ascetic is unknown. He developed a lifelong friendship with Antony, though they met only rarely thereafter. The young man no doubt gained much spiritual insight and wisdom from their relationship. He also developed a keen fondness for all monastics, which continued throughout his lifetime.

In due course Athanasius was ordained to the ranks of the clergy. He was made a deacon in the Church. His duties included assisting at the services and coordinating assistance to the needy. Bishop Alexander also appointed him to be his archdeacon. This meant that he was the Bishop's personal secretary and confidant, the Bishop's "right-hand man." When Alexander celebrated the liturgy, Athanasius served with him. When he traveled, Athanasius accompanied him. When he had needs, Athanasius saw to them. When matters required the Bishop's attention, Athanasius brought them. When people sought an audience with the Patriarch, Athanasius scheduled them. They were an inseparable team, working as one for the betterment of the Church.

Athanasius' early years had been encompassed by turmoil, tribulation, and triumph. There was the rebellion of Lucius, the persecution of Diocletian, and the conquest of Constantine. His personal life had been shaped by the training of his parents, the example of the martyrs, his friendship with Antony of the Desert, and the tutelage of Bishop Alexander. The virtues of faith, hope, and love had gained a strong foothold in his soul. Spiritual courage was his backbone. Although he remained short in physical stature, he had grown from a child of faith to a man of God.

Chapter Two

THE ARIANS

*"...savage wolves will come in among you and
will not spare the flock."*

Acts 20:29

For the first three centuries of its existence the Church had undergone persecution. Beginning in the time of Nero, the Roman government had attacked the Christians at various times. Persecution was not constant, but came in a series of successive waves. After Nero there was persecution in the second century during the reigns of Trajan, Antoninus Pius, and Marcus Aurelius. In the third century persecution came under Septimius Severus and later under Decius. During the fourth century the last and worst of these persecutions occurred during the fierce reign of Diocletian. But even his all-out war against Christians proved to be of no avail. In the end it was the Church of Christ that emerged victorious. Not only was persecution ended, but the Emperor himself was now a Christian. The Church had gone from being an illegal religion to the favored one.

But it seems as if the Evil One had learned a lesson. Three hundred years of pagan persecution had not been enough to destroy the Church of Christ. A new strategy was needed. No longer would attack come from without. Now it would come from within. (This was the very thing that Saint Paul had warned about in the Book of Acts.) The attack came from a group called the Arians.

Born in the year of the siege of Alexandria, Athanasius lived from age five to age fifteen under the great persecution. But it was the Arians who would trouble him for the rest of his life. The Arians would cause him to be exiled five separate times for a total of seventeen years. It was the Arians who would persecute him from inside the Church. Indeed, it was the Arians who would threaten to destroy the very Church itself. It was the Arians who would for a time seize control of the major episcopal sees of the East and even control of the Empire itself. For a time the whole world had become Arian, or so it seemed, and things looked so grim that it appeared as if Athanasius was the only leader who stood against them. This view was encapsulated into the famous Latin phrase "Athanasius contra mundum". Athanasius did indeed lead the cause against the "kingdom of this world," but he was never alone in the battle. Though not conspicuous like the Arian troublemakers, the vast majority of the clergy and the laity continued to remain loyal to the truth.

The Arians were the followers of Arius, a man whose name has gone down in infamy in the history of the Church. Arius was a priest, no less, in the city of Alexandria. He had been allied with the Meletians, but after abandoning them, he was ordained to the diaconate by Bishop Peter. When he sided with the Meletians again, Peter excommunicated him. Later Arius asked forgiveness of Peter's successor, Bishop Achillas. He was forgiven and received back into the Church. Achillas then ordained him to the priesthood and put him in charge of the Church of Baucalis. Upon Achillas' death in the year 313 A.D. Alexander was consecrated as the new bishop of the patriarchal see of Alexandria. It seems that Arius was jealous over this appointment and harbored enmity against Alexander because of it.

Arius had attractive qualities. He was a tall thin man with a rather austere appearance, well-educated, and a persuasive speaker. As pastor of the Church of Baucalis he gained a reputation for his ascetic life, his theological learning, and his skill in logic. His outward appearance, social grace, and pleasing voice gained many followers, including a number of women. But there was a less attractive side to Arius, as well. He was proud, ambitious, insincere, and cunning. For six years there was no friction between Arius and Bishop Alexander. But in 319 that changed very quickly.

One day during a gathering of the clergy, Alexander took the opportunity to teach them. His subject was the unity of the Holy Trinity. Alexander, following the ancient tradition of the Church, related how God the Son is equal to God the Father. He is very God and one in essence with the Father. He is the expression of the Father's Person, Light from Light, and the very Image of the Father's essence. To the surprise and even shock of those gathered, Arius began to contradict what the Bishop was saying. Arius said that the Son was not equal to the Father and that He did not share His Divine Essence. He went on to say that the Son was a created being like all other men and that He was subject to change and alteration. He then uttered his infamous saying (which became a byword for the early Arians): "There was a time when He was not." In other words, Arius proclaimed that there was a time when the Son of God did not exist.

Alexandrians were accustomed to debate. The presence in the city of both the secular Museum and the Catechetical School lent itself to an atmosphere of open discussion. Respectful debate among learned men could be an avenue for better understanding of the truth. The intellectual emphasis in Alexandrian Christianity tolerated, and even encouraged, speculation and diversity of opinion. There were many study groups of men and women led by learned teachers, who were looked upon as sources of wisdom, and as examples of moral living. So at first the clergy listened to Arius out of respect for another's viewpoint. But it soon became apparent that Arius' opinions were going far beyond the realm of respectful debate. Indeed, blasphemy was more the order of his words.

Arius mistakenly put worldly logic before faith. He deduced that since God was a Father, there must have been a time when He had not yet had a Son. Therefore, there was a time when God the Son did not exist. The Son was not God by nature but simply a created being, whom the Father had "adopted."

The teaching of Arius clearly opposed the teaching of the Church as well as the former masters of the Catechetical School. The great teacher Origen had proclaimed that there never was a time when God was without His Image. There never was Light without Radiance. "Let him understand well who dares to say, 'Once the Son was not,' that he is saying, 'Once Wisdom was not,' and 'Word was not,' and 'Life was not.'"[2] And likewise Theognostus had explained, "The essence of the Son is not one procured from without, nor accruing out of nothing, but it sprang from the Father's essence, as the radiance of light."[3]

At first Bishop Alexander tried to be conciliatory. He hoped to convince Arius of the error of his beliefs. The Bishop rightly understood that the Church's doctrines of faith were inviolable. They were not something to be tampered with by each new generation. Rather, the duty of every generation was to preserve the faith just as it had been received. Jesus Christ had entrusted the Gospel to His disciples. Their calling was to preserve and pass it on to other faithful men who also would do likewise. The truths of the Church could be defined and expounded upon, but not changed.

Arius, however, was not interested in being corrected. Instead he began making every effort to win others over to his false doctrine. He taught his blend of poison not only in his church, but also in other meeting places and assemblies. He even went from house to house spreading his "gospel." Like the serpent of old, he spoke into the ear of every Eve who would listen. His speech was full of heresy: God was not always a Father; the Son did not always exist; though called God, the Son is God in name only; the essences of the Father and of the Son and of the Holy Spirit are separate in nature, estranged, disconnected, and alien to each other, and utterly different from each other in nature and glory. In time Arius began to gain followers even from the ranks of the clergy. From a small spark of heresy a great fire began to rage. Alexander realized that stronger measures were needed to curb it.

In 321 Bishop Alexander convened a council to deal with Arius. About one hundred bishops from Egypt and Libya attended. The council excommunicated Arius and deposed him from the clergy, along with his followers. Arius and all those who embraced his godless impiety were anathematized. Yet this did not put an end to the Arians. They continued to foment rebellion against the Church, as if they had never been censured. They devised clever arguments, and selectively quoted Scripture to seduce the simple, using their own special brand of "logic" in order to persuade others to join them. In short, they seemed to bring their attack against God Himself. As Alexander said, "They have had the audacity to rend the seamless garment of Christ, which the soldiers dared not divide."[4] Despite being disciplined by the Church, the Arians continued to spread their heresy. Several bishops sided with them, including Eusebius of Nicomedia. Eusebius expressed his support in a letter to Arius, saying, "Since your sentiments are good, pray that all may adopt them. For it is plain to anyone, that what has been made was not before its origination; but what came to be has a beginning of being."[5]

In time Eusebius became the ringleader of the Arian movement. (He is not to be confused with Eusebius of Caesarea, the Church historian, who, though siding with the Arians, was not their leader.) In him the Arians had a powerful ally. As the bishop of the imperial city of Nicomedia, Eusebius was held in favor by the Emperor Constantine. He may even have been related to him. Eusebius was also very dear to Constantia, the Emperor's sister. (Later, on her deathbed, she was to beg her brother, the Emperor Constantine, to be favorable to Arius.) As a man of theological learning and leadership ability, Eusebius would remain at the helm of Arianism for a quarter of a century. He would later lead the conspiracy against Athanasius.

Following the council at Alexandria, Alexander sent out an encyclical letter to the churches throughout the Empire. It began by saying: "Now there are gone forth in this diocese, at this time, certain lawless men, enemies of Christ, teaching an apostasy, which one may justly suspect and designate as a forerunner of Antichrist."[6] The letter went on to describe the rise of Arianism and its teachings. It also announced the council's judgment and warned all to avoid these "enemies of God and destroyers of souls." The letter was signed by sixteen priests and twenty-four deacons of Alexandria and by eighteen priests and twenty deacons of neighboring Mareotis.

Athanasius' name is listed with those deacons of Alexandria who signed the letter. However, he played a more prominent part in the proceedings than just the signing of his name. As Bishop Alexander's archdeacon, Athanasius would have written the letter for him. Athanasius was in the inner circle of leadership. From the beginning of the Arian controversy, he was deeply involved in the decisions of how to deal with the heresy. His book, *On the Incarnation*, revealed just how profound his understanding was of the Holy Trinity and the Incarnation of our Lord. Though just in his twenties, Athanasius' judgment was already highly valued. There is no doubt that he and the Bishop, along with others in the inner circle of the Alexandrian clergy, spent many a night together, agonizing over the rise of Arianism and how to deal with it.

Meanwhile, after his judgment, Arius fled to Palestine. There he wrote Eusebius of Nicomedia complaining about his treatment and reiterating his blasphemy that "the Son has a beginning, but that God is without a beginning."[7] Eusebius then invited Arius to join him in Nicomedia. Eusebius also wrote Bishop Alexander to try to persuade him to receive Arius back into communion. In support of the Arian cause he sent many letters to other bishops as well. While at Nicomedia, Arius composed his song for banquets entitled *Thalia*. Besides being a catchy showcase for Arian heresy, it also revealed just how much Arius thought of himself. It read in part:

> According to faith of God's elect, God's prudent ones,
> Holy children, rightly dividing, God's Holy Spirit receiving,
> Have I learned this from the partakers of wisdom,
> Accomplished, divinely taught, and wise in all things,
> Along their track, have I been walking, with these opinions,
> I the very famous, the much suffering for God's glory,
> And taught of God, I have acquired wisdom and knowledge.[8]

The controversy continued. Sides were taken. Letters flew. Councils were held. Even the common man in the street was engaged in debate. From every corner people argued whether or not "there was a time when He was not." All this came soon enough to the attention of Emperor Constantine. As a soldier he had worked long and fought hard to unite the Empire. As a Christian leader he desired unity in the Church just as much. But influenced by Eusebius, Constantine failed in the beginning to understand the gravity of the Arian teaching. He wrote a letter to both Alexander and Arius, exhorting them to put aside their differences and restore mutual harmony. He thought the cause of their differences to be of "a truly insignificant character and quite unworthy of such contention." (This was a far cry from Athanasius' sentiment that "this heresy has come forth upon the earth like some great monster."[9]) Peace seemed to be more on Constantine's mind than the possible consequences of an unchecked heresy. He exhorted the participants to "give me back my days of calm."[10] The letter was delivered to Alexandria by the Emperor's good friend, Bishop Hosius of Cordova.

In addition to delivering the letter from Constantine, Hosius also attempted to personally intervene in the controversy. He tried to persuade both parties to come to some kind of agreement in order to restore peace to the Church. However, both his efforts and those of Constantine came to no avail. Bishop Alexander was not about to receive Arius back until he repented, and Arius was not about to repent.

Hosius returned to the Emperor and reported that the two sides could not be reconciled. Things were at an impasse. Peace in the Church seemed far off. Bishop Hosius then proposed a possible solution to Constantine. He recommended to the Emperor that a council of the entire Church be convened to deal with the controversy. Constantine liked the proposal and agreed to fund the necessary expenses. Bishops and other representatives of the Church from throughout the Empire were asked to journey to Nicea to meet in council. This gathering was to be the First Ecumenical Council of the Church.

CHAPTER THREE

THE COUNCIL OF NICEA

"…no prophecy of Scripture is of any private interpretation,
for prophecy never came by the will of man, but holy men of
God spoke as they were moved by the Holy Spirit."

2 Peter 1:20-21

The idea of a council was not something new. In fact, the first council of the Church is recorded in the Book of Acts. When the New Testament Church began, the first converts to Christianity came from the Jewish people. It was to the Jews first that Jesus Christ had come. From Old Testament times they had enjoyed a special covenant relationship with God. To them the much awaited Messiah had now appeared in the Person of Jesus Christ. But Jesus came not just for the people of Israel but for all people. Thus as the Gospel spread, the Church increasingly began to receive Gentiles into the faith. The question then arose of just how they should be received.

Gentile converts came to the Church without the Jewish inheritance of faith. Often they came from paganism directly into the Church. Was it necessary then for them to adopt the Jewish laws of the Old Covenant? Some Church leaders felt that it was necessary. Others felt that it was not. To resolve this issue a council was held at Jerusalem in the year A.D. 50. After vigorously debating the issue, the leaders of the Church reached a consensus. James, the Bishop of Jerusalem, summed up their agreement when he said that it was not necessary for the Gentiles who were turning to God to keep the Old Testament Jewish laws but that they should abstain from things polluted by idols, from sexual immorality, from things strangled, and from blood. In proclaiming their decision, the Council of Jerusalem wrote: "For it seemed good to the Holy Spirit, and to us, to lay upon you no greater burden than these necessary things." (Ac 15:28)

The pattern was set. From the earliest times Church decisions were made in council. The understanding of the Church was that through such councils the will of God would be revealed through the inspiration of the Holy Spirit. The bishop and the presbytery constituted such a gathering on the local level. On a regional level a council was made up of a synod of bishops. For the first three centuries of the Church such councils met to resolve theological issues, as well as to determine matters of discipline. Various local councils had been held at different times, but an ecumenical council, a council of the whole Church, had never before been held.

The First Ecumenical Council of the Church was held in the year 325 in the city of Nicea in Bithynia of Asia Minor. The most distinguished leaders of the Church assembled there from throughout the Roman Empire; from Africa, Asia, and Europe. Over three hundred bishops attended. Along with them came a great number of priests, deacons, and others who swelled the ranks of those in attendance to nearly two thousand. Due to the location of the Council, most attendants were from the East. But all parts of the West were represented.

From every corner of the Empire they came: from Syria, Cilicia, Phoenicia, Arabia, Palestine, Egypt, Pontus, Galatia,

Cappadocia, Pamphylia, Thrace, Macedonia, Greece, Italy, Spain, Gaul, and Britain. From the four ancient apostolic sees came the Patriarchs: Macarius of Jerusalem, Eustathius of Antioch, the presbyters, Vito and Vicentius, representing the aged Sylvester of Rome, and Alexander of Alexandria. In Alexander's entourage were fourteen auxiliary bishops and other leaders, along with a particularly interesting young man of small stature, but with a handsome and animated face: the archdeacon Athanasius. Though not yet a bishop, Athanasius was held in the first rank of the members of the Council, due to his wisdom and virtue, which were well beyond his years.

Many notable hierarchs attended. Among these were: the venerable Hosius of Cordova in Spain, who persuaded Constantine to convene the Council; Paphnutius of Thebes, the wonder worker; Spiridon of Cyprus; Potammon of Heracles, who had lost an eye in Maximin's persecution; Paul of Neocaesarea, whose hands had been paralyzed with red-hot irons under the persecution of Licinius; James of Nisibis, the great saint of Mesopotamia; Arisdaghes of Armenia, the son of Gregory the Illuminator; John of Persia, from a Church which could trace its origin to sub-apostolic missionaries; Leontius of Cappadocia; Hypatius of Gangra, afterwards murdered by heretics; Marcellus of Ancyra, a determined supporter of Bishop Alexander; Alexander of Byzantium; Peoderos of Heraclea; Pistus of Athens; Alexander of Thessalonica, a venerable man held in high esteem; Protogenes of Sardica; Theophilus, bishop of the Goths; Capito of Sicily; Nicholas of Myra; Marcus of Calabria; and Domnus of Stridon. The allies of Arius included: Theognius of Nicea, Maris of Chalcedon, Menophantus of Ephesus, Theonas of Marmarica, Eusebius of Caesarea, and Eusebius of Nicomedia, the leader of the Arian party.

Before the Council was officially convened depositions were taken. Arius and his followers were summoned before the assembly. They were given an opportunity to present their theology. During the meetings many of the Orthodox clergy powerfully refuted the Arian arguments. Some quickly gained notice for their skill in opposing the heresy and in proclaiming the true faith. One of those who gained special notice was Athanasius. His understanding of the divinity of Christ was already well set forth in his book, *Against the Gentiles*, where he wrote: "He is the very Wisdom, very Word, and very own Power of the Father, very Light, very Truth, very Righteousness, very Virtue, and in truth His express Image, and Brightness, and Resemblance. And to sum it up, He is the wholly perfect Fruit of the Father, and He is alone the Son, and unchanging Image of the Father."[11]

The Council officially began in June. Proceedings began with the arrival of the Emperor Constantine. He addressed the assembly and encouraged them towards the restoration of harmony. He gave thanks to God for seeing so many of the clergy of the Church gathered together into one place. His desire, he said, was for them to be of one mind and of one judgment. He considered dissension within the Church to be the most dangerous of all evils. The root of this disturbance he believed was the Evil One himself. No longer being able to persecute the Church from without, he was now seeking to disturb the Church from within. He asked all the bishops present to put a peaceful end to the strife. To punctuate his desire he made a public demonstration. Certain petitions had been brought to him by various participants of the Council. Most of these petitions contained private grievances, along with the hope that the Emperor would rule in their favor. Constantine asked that these petitions be brought into the assembly. He then had them publicly burned.

Because of the seriousness of the Arian heresy and its threat to the Church, passions ran high and debates were heated. Arius was often called in to explain his views. It soon became apparent to most of the bishops that his views were simply heretical. The Arians, perhaps sensing their condemnation, tried to be as evasive as possible. Like chameleons (as Bishop Alexander said) they kept altering their arguments. During the debates they were seen whispering and winking to one another with regard to terms being used to describe the Son's equality with the Father. When the bishops stated that the Son was the Image of the Father, the Arians replied that they could agree to this "for even man is made in His image." When it was said that Christ is the Power of God, they replied that "even the caterpillar and the locust are called the power of God." And so on. The Arians could agree that the Son was like the Father, but they refused to confess that the Son was consubstantial (of the same essence) with the Father. They said He was of "like essence" ("homoiousion" in Greek) with God the Father, but not of the "same essence" ("homoousion" in Greek) as the Father.

Eusebius of Nicomedia presented a statement of the Arian faith for the Council. It was read and the contents were immediately declared to be spurious and false. The paper was torn to shreds. Eusebius of Caesarea presented a creed which sounded orthodox but left out the word "consubstantial," which left the door open for an Arian interpretation. It was evident to the Council that no statement of faith would be adequate without the word "homoousion." Anything less would not do.

The Council carefully formulated a statement of faith which was eventually signed by 318 bishops. It declared the Son to be the Only-begotten of the Father, not made, but consubstantial ("homoousios") with the Father. An anathema was laid on those who refused to acknowledge the Son to be consubstantial with the Father. When the Arians protested that the word "homoousion" was not to be found in Scripture, the bishops replied that neither was the Arian catch-phrase "there was a time when he was not." The bishops had not dreamed up some new term, but simply used the word "consubstantial" to precisely state the faith which the Church had always believed. The Creed of the Nicene Council read thus:

> We believe in one God, the Father Almighty, Maker of all things, visible and invisible; and in one Lord Jesus Christ, the Son of God, the only-begotten of the Father, that is of the substance of the Father; God of God and Light of Light; true God of true God; begotten, not made, consubstantial with the Father: by Whom all things were made, both which are in heaven and on earth: Who for the sake of us men, and on account of our salvation, descended, became incarnate, and was made man; suffered, arose again on the third day, and ascended into the heavens, and will come again to judge the living and the dead. We also believe in the Holy Spirit. But the holy Catholic and Apostolic church anathematizes those who say "There was a time when He was not" and "He was not before He was begotten" and "He was made from that which did not exist" and those who assert that He is of other substance or essence than the Father, or that He was created, or is susceptible of change.[12] (Further refinements to the Creed were later made by the Second Ecumenical Council at Constantinople in 381 A.D.)

When the Arians saw that their cause was lost, many of them

began to abandon ranks. Soon there were only five left who refused to sign the Creed: Eusebius of Nicomedia, Theognius of Nicea, Maris of Chalcedon, Theonas of Marmarica, and Secundus of Ptolemais. But in the end only two held out: Theonas and Secundus. Even Eusebius the leader of the movement acquiesced. Thus, most of the Arians at the Council signed the Creed and publicly renounced Arius. Their action, however, was motivated by convenience rather than conviction. Time would soon show their true colors. Arius, Theonas and Secundus were exiled by the Emperor. (A precedent which would later prove to be fateful for Athanasius himself.) The Council excommunicated Arius and those who adhered to his doctrine.

The Council's work, however, was not yet complete. Other issues besides the Arian controversy also needed attention. For the next two months the Council continued to meet. The calculation for determining the date of Easter was standardized. (Previous to this, the date of Holy Pascha had been set according to local custom, which sometimes varied from place to place.) The Meletian schism was also dealt with. The Meletians, who had founded a parallel church structure within parts of Egypt, were given leniency, grace being the overall medicine applied. (This grace, in the years that followed, would be taken advantage of by the Meletians when they later sided with the Arians.) Finally the Council handed down twenty canons which dealt with Church discipline and order. The Council sent a letter to the churches of Alexandria and Egypt officially informing them of their decisions, especially their condemnation of Arius and his followers. The Emperor Constantine sent letters to all those bishops who were not able to attend the Council, encouraging them toward unity of faith and mutual love. In August the bishops and the other participants returned home with the best wishes of the Emperor.

The First Ecumenical Council had come to an end. Its influence, however, was to be long lasting. Called by Constantine to quell the Arian controversy, the Council of Nicea bequeathed to the Church a most wonderful and precise definition of the divinity of Christ. The relationship of God the Father to God the Son is something which cannot be adequately explained with words, yet the creed of the Council had done precisely that. Few could argue whether the Holy Spirit was with the Council. Their statement of Christology has continued to be embraced by the Church throughout the centuries. Arianism had been exposed for what it was: an insidious heresy. Arius and his followers had been condemned. The bishops, who had so wonderfully expressed the true apostolic faith, must have felt that the Arian controversy was now over. On the contrary, it had only begun.

Chapter Four

THE NEW BISHOP

"For a bishop, as God's steward, must be blameless, not self-willed,
not quick-tempered, not given to wine, not violent,
not greedy for money, but hospitable, a lover of what is good,
temperate, just, holy, self-controlled, holding fast the faithful word
as he has been taught, that he may be able both to exhort with
sound doctrine and to refute those who contradict it."

Titus 1:7-9

When the Council of Nicea concluded, Bishop Alexander began his journey home. His fellow clergy, including his trusted archdeacon Athanasius, traveled with him. Egypt had been well represented at the proceedings. Many bishops, priests, and deacons had attended. The participants had come from Alexandria and from all parts of Egypt. Their attendance and vigorous participation at the Council had been especially valuable, since it was in their homeland that Arius had first put forth his heresy. The leadership of Alexander, and his beloved Athanasius, in combating Arianism had been crucial. Years of struggle and debate for the truth had finally been vindicated by the decision of the Council. Arianism was declared to be a heresy. Its cause was overthrown, and Arius and those with him were condemned. A great struggle had been engaged in and truth was the victor.

At the conclusion of the Council, the Synod of Bishops at Nicea sent an official letter to the Church of Alexandria and to all the brethren throughout Egypt, Libya, and Pentapolis. The letter included an exhortation for the people to rejoice in the conclusions of the Council, in the oneness of mind, in the peace of the accord, and in the destruction of heresy. The letter concluded with a personal word about their Bishop:

> Receive with great honor and more abundant love our fellow-minister and your Bishop, Alexander, who has greatly delighted us by his presence, and even at his advanced age has undergone extraordinary exertions in order that peace might be re-established among you. Pray on behalf of us all, that the things decided as just be inviolably maintained through Almighty God, and our Lord Jesus Christ, together with the Holy Spirit, to Whom be glory for ever. Amen.[13]

The great struggle for truth had taken its toll upon Patriarch Alexander. His health declined and he continued to remain in poor health for the next two and a half years. When Alexander realized that he was nearing the end of his life, he made known his choice for his successor. The one whom he most trusted to succeed him was Athanasius. Alexander's choice was a logical one. It was also a choice from the heart. Alexander had known Athanasius from his boyhood. He had watched him mature and grow from a youth, to a student, to a disciple, to an author, to a trusted confidant, to an archdeacon, to a fellow fighter against Arianism, to a respected participant at Nicea. He was no longer the youth that he had first met fifteen years earlier. His time had come. He was now ready to assume the office of bishop.

On his deathbed Alexander called for Athanasius. The deacon, however, was not to be found. He had left the city. Apparently, out of humility, he had sought to avoid the honor of the episcopate. Another deacon by the same name answered the bishop's call. However, Alexander did not respond to him, for he was calling for the archdeacon Athanasius. Then realizing that Athanasius was away, Alexander prophetically exclaimed, "O Athanasius, you think to escape, but you will not."[14]

Popular opinion was behind the Bishop's choice. Many people clamored for Athanasius' election, referring to him as "the good, the pious, a Christian, one of the ascetics, a genuine bishop."[15] The bishops of Egypt and Libya also agreed with Bishop Alexander's choice. After Bishop Alexander's death, they elected Athanasius as the new Bishop. He was consecrated the Patriarch of Alexandria on June 8, 328, being just thirty years of age (the minimum canonical age for the episcopate).

The episcopal see to which Athanasius succeeded was the second in prominence in all Christendom (Rome being the first). The Patriarch of Alexandria had direct jurisdiction over all the bishops of Egypt and Libya. The local clergy, of course, tended to the cycles of prayer and to the day to day matters of the churches, but to all of them the Patriarch acted as a father. And, thus, like bishops of other major sees in ancient times he was commonly addressed as Pope (or Papa). Not only did the Patriarch oversee spiritual matters, but he also was in charge of the distribution of funds for the support of the churches and for the help of the poor. Thus, the office came with a considerable amount of power and an equally considerable amount of responsibility.

One of the customary tasks for the Patriarch was to write a Paschal Letter each year. This letter was written prior to Lent. Copies of it were sent to all the churches under the Patriarch's jurisdiction. The purpose of the letter, first of all, was to announce the date for Pascha (Easter) and the beginning of Lent. Secondly, it gave the Bishop an opportunity to teach and exhort the people of God. As the new Patriarch, Athanasius wrote his first Paschal Letter in the year 329. The letter contains the first extant recorded words of Athanasius in his new office as Bishop.

In his letter Athanasius said that at this season the Sun of Righteousness causes His divine rays to shine on us once again. We ought then to be sure, he warned, to celebrate this time. Otherwise, when this season has passed by, joy might pass us by as well. Just as the sound of a trumpet called together the nation of Israel, so the season of Lent trumpets forth the coming of the Feast of Pascha. The trumpet call is a signal as well as a warning. We should hallow the fast and not pollute it. We should avoid evil thoughts in our hearts, evil actions against our neighbor, and the exaltation of ourselves above others. A true fast involves both the body and the soul. The body is to fast from food, while the soul is to fast from wickedness. Let us then cast away all hypocrisy and fraud, he added, and put far from us all pride and deceit, and let us take up love for God and our neighbor. In this way we may someday "pass to the place of the wondrous tabernacle, to the house of God; with the voice of gladness and thanksgiving, the shouting of those who rejoice; where pain and sorrow and sighing have fled, and upon our hearts gladness and joy shall have come to us! May we be judged worthy to be partakers in these things."[16]

One of Athanasius' first efforts as Bishop was to visit the many churches of Egypt. His desire was to both encourage and strengthen the people of God. Traveling south, his first visits were in the Thebaid. From there he traveled up the Nile as far as Aswan.

Pope Athanasius visited both churches and monasteries along the way. When he came to the monks of Pachomius, everyone went out to meet him, as was the custom. They escorted the Bishop to the monastery with the chanting of psalms. Once there he addressed the monks, encouraged them, and prayed in the church. Then he visited each monk's cell. At this point Apa Sarapion, Bishop of Nitentori, grasped Athanasius' hand and begged the Patriarch to ordain Pachomius as a priest. Pachomius, wishing to avoid this honor, disappeared in the crowd of monks. When Athanasius had been seated and the great crowd with him, he said, "Indeed, I have learned about the renown of the faith of this man Apa Pachomius of whom you speak to me, since I have been at Alexandria and even before my consecration." Then he arose, prayed, and said to the brothers, "Greet your father, and say to him, 'So, you hid from us, fleeing from that which leads to jealousy, discord, and envy, and you chose for yourself that which is better and which will always abide in Christ! Our Lord, therefore, will accede to your wish.'"[17] Then the Patriarch departed, accompanied by a great crowd carrying lamps, candles, and censers.

Back in Alexandria Athanasius helped a young man, named Theodore, along the spiritual path, just as Bishop Alexander had once helped him. Though raised as a pagan, Theodore was moved by God to become a Christian. He went to the Bishop and told him everything that was in his heart. After a period of instruction he was baptized and made a lector or reader. Athanasius provided a place for him to live at the church. There Theodore began to lead an ascetic life. The *Pachomian Koinonia* records that "he led a great way of life as far as his strength allowed, finding himself near the source of fresh and living water, that is, the apostolic archbishop Apa Athanasius."[18]

While Athanasius was busy with the duties of the episcopate, his enemies were also busy with the plotting of schemes. For a time after the Council, the Arians had been scattered. Their leaders had either been exiled or fallen out of favor. But this situation did not last long. Within the first year of Athanasius' episcopate, Eusebius of Nicomedia had managed to get himself restored to the Emperor's favor and was once again bending Constantine's ear. Though the Arian cause had been weakened, it was not dead, and Eusebius meant to revive it. He began to work in every way possible to undo the decisions of Nicea. To accomplish this he came up with a twofold plan. First, he wanted to get Arius restored to communion in Alexandria and, second, he wanted to get Athanasius removed from his see. To accomplish this, Eusebius used many promises to gain the support of the Meletians in Egypt. Together they formed an alliance to oppose Athanasius.

Eusebius managed to convince the Emperor to bring Arius back from exile. Eusebius then wrote to Athanasius demanding that Arius be restored to communion. His letter was full of threats. If Athanasius refused to comply, he said that there would be dire consequences. Naturally, Athanasius refused. Another letter followed. This time the letter came from the Emperor himself. Constantine ordered Patriarch Athanasius to admit Arius to communion at once. If he refused to do so the Emperor proclaimed, "I will immediately send someone who shall depose you."[19]

Athanasius did not budge. He responded in a letter to Constantine that anti-Christian heresy has no place within the Church of God. Eusebius then sent three Meletian bishops to appear before the Emperor. This evil trio brought false charges against Athanasius. They claimed that he had exacted a tax upon Egyptians to pay for the expenses of the Church, and that they were the first "victims" of this tax. Providentially, two presbyters from Alexandria were at the court at this same time. They quickly disproved this false charge. The Meletian trio then received a stern rebuke from Constantine. But the Meletians were not done. They laid other charges against the Patriarch. They said that he was under the canonical age of thirty when he was consecrated bishop, that he governed with arrogance and violence, that he used magic, and that he supported persons who were guilty of treason against the state. How much stock Constantine took in these ridiculous charges is uncertain, but he did summon Athanasius to appear before him in order to answer them.

Dutifully, Athanasius departed for Constantinople late in the year 330. After arriving at Constantinople, he appeared before the Emperor. He successfully refuted all the charges that had been brought against him. Matters went slowly, however. By the time that he was completely exonerated of all the charges, he was stricken by a lengthy illness and was unable to travel. When his health did improve, his departure was further delayed by unfavorable winter weather. However, he was able to send the customary Paschal Letter to his beloved flock:

> I send to you, my beloved, late and beyond the accustomed time [this letter]. Yet I trust you will forgive the delay, on account of my protracted journey, and because I have been tried with illness. Being hindered by these two causes and unusually severe storms having occurred, I have deferred writing to you. But notwithstanding my long journeys, and my grievous sickness, I have not forgotten to give you the festal notification, and in discharge of my duty, I now announce to you the feast. For although this letter is later than usual for this announcement, it should be considered well-timed, since our enemies having been put to shame and reproved by the Church, because they persecuted us without a cause, we may now sing a festal song of praise,

uttering the triumphant hymn of praise against Pharaoh: "We will sing unto the Lord, for He is to be gloriously praised; the horse and rider He has cast into the sea."[20]

When the weather improved Athanasius sailed for Alexandria. He returned joyously to his people. In his possession he carried with him a letter to the Church of Alexandria from the Emperor. It exonerated him of all charges. In condemning those who falsely accused the Patriarch, Constantine wrote: "Those wretches have no power against your bishop. Believe me, brethren, their endeavors will have no effect other than this, after they have worn down our days, to leave for themselves no place for repentance in this life."[21]

Athanasius did not arrive back home until early in the year 332. Lent was already half over. He had been gone more than one year.

CHAPTER FIVE

INTRIGUE

"Why do the nations rage, and the people plot in vain?"
Psalm 2:1

The Arian-Meletian alliance had not accomplished its goal. Athanasius was still the Patriarch of Alexandria. Though he had been forced to appear in person before Constantine, he was able to answer the charges made against him. He effectively refuted these charges and was judged to be innocent of them. Though he had been kept away from his beloved flock and homeland for over a year, now he was back home once again performing his sacred duties. The accusations of the Arians had been shown to be false, and for their efforts they had incurred a rebuke from the Emperor. Their cause had been embarrassed, and their actions must have seemed ridiculous to many, but they were not ones to give up easily. Indeed, Athanasius had aptly nicknamed them the "Ariomaniacs," for their maniacal devotion to their heretical cause. Even though the charges against the blessed Bishop Athanasius had been dismissed, the Arians continued to plot and scheme against him. In the months that followed, their perseverance gave birth to two new accusations. They were serious ones.

The first of these involved the case of Ischyras, who was from the small village of Irene Secontaruri. Ischyras had been ordained to the priesthood by a certain schismatic priest named Colluthus. Though he was not a bishop, Colluthus had taken upon himself to ordain followers. The Alexandrian council of 324 had pronounced his ordinations invalid. This meant that Ischyras was actually not a priest at all. But in spite of the judgment of the council, Ischyras still acted as a priest. He continued to hold services in his village. His place of worship was a tiny cottage. His "parishioners" were seven inhabitants of the village. They were all his relatives.

During a visit to the area, Bishop Athanasius learned of Ischyras' charade. He was concerned about the matter and sent the priest Macarius to find Ischyras. Macarius was instructed to bring Ischyras before the Bishop for questioning.

When Macarius arrived at the village, he found Ischyras sick in bed. He was too ill to travel. The best Macarius could do was to tell Ischyras' father that his son should cease masquerading as a priest. This admonition was ignored. When Ischyras regained his health, he continued to imitate the priesthood. He also joined himself with the schismatic Meletians. It was sometime after this that a story was concocted about Macarius' visit. Ischyras accused the priest Macarius of using physical violence against him and in the process breaking a communion chalice in his "church." This accusation was forwarded by the Meletians to Eusebius, who encouraged them to "develop" it. The story then began to take on a life of its own. Ischyras, it seems, had now been celebrating the liturgy when Macarius arrived, and not only was the holy chalice broken but the altar itself had been overturned.

Under pressure from his relatives, however, Ischyras recanted his story and apologized to Athanasius in person. He came to the Patriarch in tears confessing that the entire story was false. He left with Athanasius a written confession. It stated that the Meletians had coerced him, and even physically beaten him, into bringing the false accusation. Though Athanasius forgave Ischyras for his misdeeds, he still felt it necessary to censure him. Shortly after this, Ischyras revived his accusation all over again. Perhaps, he became bitter over his censure or he was simply a double-minded man. The new version of the story held that it was the Patriarch himself who had broken the cup. The altar which had been overturned now became a large church which the Bishop had supposedly ordered to be torn down. The accusation in its final form was spread abroad by the Arians, and then brought to the Emperor.

The second accusation that was brought against Athanasius was the case of Arsenius. Arsenius was a Meletian bishop of Hypsele. He was given a large bribe by John Arcaph. (John Arcaph was the leader of the schismatic Meletians. On his deathbed Meletius had consecrated John to be his successor. This violated the terms of the Council of Nicea, which directed Meletius to cease ordaining clergy.) The purpose of the bribe was to get Arsenius to go into hiding. He traveled into the desert of the Thebaid. Arriving at Ptermenkurkis, he was hidden away by some Meletian monks. Once Arsenius was out of sight, John quickly started a rumor that Athanasius had murdered him. In addition, it was said that one of Arsenius' hands had been cut from his corpse and that the Patriarch was using this severed hand for magical purposes. The Meletians even produced a severed hand and claimed it to be the very one in question. A report of this fabrication was sent to Constantine. Troubled by this latest accusation, Constantine directed his half-brother, Dalmatius of Antioch, to check into the matter. Dalmatius made an inquiry and suggested that a council be held. It was to be at Caesarea in the year 334. Eusebius, Bishop of Caesarea (not the same Eusebius as that of Nicomedia) was to preside. Athanasius strongly protested. He knew he would not get a fair trial before Eusebius, who was in the company of the Arians.

Accordingly, the council was moved from Caesarea to Tyre and postponed until the year 335. The Emperor Constantine appointed Count Flavius Dionysius to represent him there and to assure that the proceedings were held in fairness. Athanasius was ordered to appear before the council.

Meanwhile, the Patriarch summoned one of his trusted deacons and sent him on a mission to find Arsenius. The deacon became a detective. He was able to trace Arsenius to the Meletian monks in the nome (province) of Antaeopolis in Upper Egypt. However, before he could get there, Pinnes, a Meletian priest, learned of the search. Pinnes acted quickly. He directed the monk Helias to smuggle Arsenius down the Nile. From there Arsenius sailed to Tyre. Meanwhile, the deacon and a number of men with him came upon the Meletians. Pinnes was arrested and taken to Alexandria. There the monk Helias was also found. Both were taken before the authorities. Both confessed to the plot.

By now Arsenius had successfully reached Tyre. But he was not very clever about hiding. He chose a public inn for his place of refuge. A servant of the city magistrate soon learned that he was there. The magistrate arrested Arsenius and had Athanasius informed. At first, it seems, Arsenius denied that he was himself. This charade did not last long, because the Bishop of Tyre knew him by sight and easily identified him. Arsenius was then proven to be who he was — a scoundrel. Once identified, he confessed and admitted to his guilt. (John Arcaph, the ringleader of the plot, also later admitted his guilt and renounced the Meletian cause, but his renunciation was only temporary, and he soon returned to his former ways.) When Constantine was informed of the latest twist of events, he expressed indignation over the whole affair. It would then have seemed to serve no good purpose for Athanasius to still appear before the council. But the Emperor, perhaps hoping that the council might bring a final end to the whole troublesome matter, allowed the investigations to proceed. Arsenius, meanwhile, was kept in custody by Athanasius' supporters.

Being summoned to appear before the council, Athanasius departed from Alexandria in July and journeyed to Tyre. From the beginning things did not bode well for the Patriarch. The influence of the Arians was very strong. They outnumbered the supporters of Athanasius by two to one. The bishop who was chosen to preside over the council was the Arian Eusebius of Caesarea. The whole atmosphere was very intense. There was enough concern for order that Count Dionysius ordered a military guard to stand by.

Emotions ran high as the proceedings began. Discussions were heated. Accusations flew. The Arians regurgitated every possible charge against Athanasius. The chief one was that he had used violence and force. The number of false witnesses who testified against him, and the willingness of the majority to believe them, left Athanasius with profound misgivings as to any possibility of a fair hearing. The Patriarch objected to the council that some of the bishops assembled to judge his case were clearly biased against him. In addition, the bishops of Egypt also protested against the testimony of Meletian witnesses, who were Arian allies.

At this point, however, the Arians outdid themselves. They brought up the case of Arsenius. Unaware that Arsenius was being held in custody, they once again proclaimed that he had been murdered by the order of Athanasius. One of them even brought forth the "severed hand" as evidence. The hand made quite an impression on the council, but Athanasius was poised for the moment. Arsenius, who had been kept under guard, was now ushered in. He was, obviously, alive and well. At this point many at the synod apparently expected some explanation to follow as to how Arsenius had lost his hand. Arsenius was wrapped in a cloak. Athanasius then lifted up the cloak and revealed a hand. Then pausing for a moment while the suspense built, he lifted up the cloak further and showed the assembly that Arsenius had a second hand as well. Then he pronounced, "Arsenius, as you see, has two hands. Let my accusers show the place where the third was cut off."[22] This was too much for John Arcaph, who immediately fled the scene. But the rest of the Eusebian party remained unfazed. They claimed that some sort of magic was involved. Certainly, Athanasius was at least guilty of attempted murder, they said. Poor Arsenius had simply hid himself out of fear. No, the accused would not be cleared so easily.

Next the majority decided that a commission should be appointed to investigate the case of Ischyras. The commission would travel to Alexandria, gather evidence, and bring back a report. Over the objections of Athanasius, all those chosen for the task were Arians or Arian sympathizers. Indeed, even Ischyras himself was to accompany them. Those accused in the matter, Athanasius and Macarius, had to remain at Tyre. The Egyptian bishops protested to Count Dionysius that the commission was clearly biased. Dionysius advised Eusebius that fairness was in order, but his words had no effect. Athanasius, realizing that justice would not be forthcoming, decided to take his case directly to the Emperor. Departing the city at night, he sailed for Constantinople in an open boat, along with four of his trusted bishops.

Meanwhile couriers from the council were sent to Egypt to gather "witnesses" for the commission. They were given a four day head-start. When the commission arrived at Alexandria, they were assisted by the prefect Philagrius, an Arian sympathizer. The commission refused to allow the clergy or the laity of the Church to testify. Though they continued to insist that they be allowed to take part in the proceedings, none of them were called as witnesses. In response to this, the clergy drafted a letter of protest to the commission and sent a copy of it to the Controller Palladius, but it was to no avail. Instead the commission brought forward catechumens, and even Jews and pagans, for questioning (the very people who would know the least about the matter in question). These "witnesses" were prompted to give certain answers. Those who failed to give the "correct" answers were threatened by Philagrius' soldiers. The especially dull were prodded with swords. Yet in spite of all this, the commission did not get all that it had hoped for. Much of the contrived testimony was contradictory. Some of it actually favored Athanasius. Philagrius became frustrated over this and took out his frustration on the nuns of the city. He incited a heathen mob which beat, mocked, and ill-treated them.

Armed with the shoddy evidence that they had gathered, the commission then traveled back to Tyre. There they presented their report to the council. Apparently, their findings suited the Arians just fine. Having the majority vote, they condemned Athanasius and deposed him from his see.

By this time Patriarch Athanasius and his fellow bishops had arrived at port outside Constantinople. It was now October. They immediately set out on foot toward the imperial city. As it turned out, they did not have to reach the city in order to see the Emperor. As they were walking down the road in one direction, who should be coming toward them in the opposite direction, but Constantine himself. He was on horseback with an entourage.

When Athanasius recognized him, he dispensed with the usual protocol. He stood in the middle of the road, directly in the Emperor's path. As Constantine drew near, the Bishop called out, requesting an audience. The Emperor did not recognize him at first, and he was startled by the sudden encounter. He was not used to being addressed so abruptly and was not pleased about it. Constantine's attendants soon identified Athanasius, but the Emperor refused to speak to him. Athanasius asked again to be heard. Constantine's patience had worn thin. He was just about to order that the Bishop be physically removed, when Athanasius boldly asked for just one favor. He asked that the bishops at the council of Tyre be summoned to the court so that he might have the opportunity to defend himself against their charges in the Emperor's presence. This seemed to Constantine to be a reasonable request. He granted it. The bishops from the council at Tyre were summoned.

When the imperial summons from the Emperor arrived at Tyre, the leaders of the Arian cause instructed the rest of their allies to go home. Eusebius of Nicomedia and his inner circle of Arian bishops would represent them. (The other bishops were Theognius, Patrophilus, Ursacius, Valens, and Eusebius of Caesarea.) By the time they arrived at court they had developed a new strategy. Gone were the old charges against Athanasius. A new one had been concocted. The Patriarch was now accused of threatening to starve the city of Constantinople by stopping the grain shipments from Egypt. (In 332 Constantine had begun the free distribution of grain in the new capital city. The grain that had formerly been shipped from Alexandria to Rome was now being shipped to Constantinople.) When Athanasius protested that he did not have the power to do any such thing, Eusebius replied that the Patriarch was a rich man and he could do whatever he liked. This charge was apparently too much for Constantine. A nerve had been hit. He immediately ordered that Athanasius be banished. He was to be exiled to Gaul.

Why Constantine took this action is uncertain. There are three possibilities. First, Constantine may have actually believed the charge brought against the Patriarch. Secondly, he might have been attempting to protect Athanasius from execution. Anyone convicted of this particular charge could receive a sentence of death. (In fact, a one-time advisor to Constantine named Sopater had been executed over this very thing. He had been accused of delaying the grain shipments to Constantinople by using magic to "fetter the winds.") Third, the Emperor might have thought that he could bring peace to the Church by removing the person who was at the center of the controversy. Whatever the reason, Constantine had ruled against Athanasius. The Arians had won a victory. Their nemesis, the outspoken defender of Orthodox Christology, was now out of the way. It was to be the first of many exiles for this courageous man of God.

CHAPTER SIX

EXILE

"…in the world you will have tribulation; but be of good cheer,
I have overcome the world."

John 16:33

Athanasius was exiled to Treveri. Located in Gaul, it was on the banks of the Moselle River. Athanasius had the run of the city and was not treated as a prisoner. His "prison" was being absent from his homeland. This was sentence enough, considering how much he loved his faithful people. (He often addressed them as "my beloved" in his letters.) Others from Egypt resided with him. His needs were met, and he and Bishop Maximinus of Treveri became good friends. Athanasius was to remain in Treveri for over a year.

Even from exile Athanasius wrote and encouraged his clergy and faithful. "For although place separates us," he said, "yet the Lord, the Giver of the feast and Who is Himself our Feast, Who is also the Bestower of the Spirit, brings us together in mind, in harmony, and in the bond of peace. For when we think and care about the same things, and offer up the same prayers on behalf of each other, no place can separate us, but the Lord gathers and unites us together."[23]

The deaths of two different men were to have a great impact upon Athanasius' exile. The first death was that of Arius. When the council of Tyre ended, the assembly of bishops traveled to Jerusalem for the dedication of the Church of the Holy Sepulcher. There Arius was accepted into communion. This was done on the basis of a confession of faith that Arius had made. Letters, announcing his acceptance into communion, were sent by the synod to the Church of Egypt and to the Church at large. Arius then journeyed to Alexandria. He hoped that with the Patriarch gone he could now receive communion there as well. He was mistaken. He was no more able to receive communion at Alexandria now than he was in the past. Realizing that the situation was not going to change, Arius left for Constantinople.

When he arrived in Constantinople, Arius received an invitation to appear before the Emperor. The invitation was received through the influence of Eusebius and his allies. At their meeting Constantine asked Arius if he held to the true faith of the Church. Arius swore that he did, even producing a written confession of faith. (He conveniently withheld the points which had caused him to be excommunicated in the first place.) The Emperor was satisfied with his statement, but he added a prophetic warning: "If your faith is right, you have done well to swear to it; but if it is impious, and you have sworn, God judge you according to your oath."[24]

Eusebius and those with him then escorted Arius to the church. Alexander, the Bishop of Constantinople, however, resisted them. He said that an inventor of heresy should have no part in communion. Eusebius replied that Arius had been invited by the Emperor himself, and that whether Alexander liked it or not, Arius would receive communion the next day. Alexander was greatly dismayed over this. Full of emotion, he entered the church, and there he prostrated himself on the floor and began to pray.

He begged and implored God that either his life might be taken before he could witness such an abomination or that the life of Arius might be taken. God heard Alexander's prayer. That very night Arius and his fellows were parading through the city. They were celebrating their victory and exalting themselves. As they did so, however, Arius suffered a sudden and violent hemorrhage of the bowels and died. His judgment had come swiftly. He lost not only the communion that he had sought, but also his life.

Upon hearing of his death, Constantine was struck with wonder on how Arius had been convicted of his perjury. Athanasius, on his part, responded with reserve at the death of his enemy. He shared his thoughts in a letter to Bishop Serapion of Egypt:

> Such has been the end of Arius. Eusebius and his fellows, overwhelmed with shame buried their accomplice, while the blessed Alexander, amidst the rejoicings of the Church, celebrated communion with piety and orthodoxy, praying with all the brethren, and greatly glorifying God, not as exulting in his death (God forbid), "for it is appointed unto all men once to die," but because this thing had been shown forth in a manner transcending human judgments. For the Lord Himself judging between the threats of Eusebius and his fellows, and the prayer of Alexander, condemned the Arian heresy, showing it to be unworthy of communion with the Church, and making manifest to all, that although it receive the support of the Emperor and of all mankind, yet it is condemned by the Church herself. So the unchristian gang of the Arian madmen has been shown to be unpleasing to God and impious.[25]

A second death was to bring Athanasius out of exile. This was the death of Constantine himself. Though Constantine had been a professing Christian for at least twenty-five years, he had never been baptized. The practice of postponing baptism was not unheard of during this era, since there was a great fear about the consequence of sin after baptism. Some held the view that sins committed after baptism could not be forgiven. As a result, some people postponed their baptism right up until their deathbed. Constantine was one of these. On his deathbed he received baptism from the hands of Eusebius. It was Sunday, May 22, 337. Within days the Emperor died.

The news of his death was quickly carried to his sons, Constantius, Constans, and Constantine II. The brothers, who had already been serving as Caesars in their respective parts of the Empire, met together at Sirmium and agreed upon a division of power. Constantius was to rule the East, Constans Italy and Illyricum, and Constantine II Gaul and Africa. When Constantine II had departed Gaul for Sirmium, he brought Athanasius out of exile with him. In a June letter to the Church of Alexandria Constantine II said that his father had exiled the Patriarch only to preserve his life and that he had always intended to restore him to his see. He said that he was fulfilling his father's wishes by sending Athanasius back to Egypt. (Whether or not this was actually his father's intention is uncertain.)

Released from exile, Patriarch Athanasius began his journey home. Passing through Constantinople and then Caesarea, he arrived back in Alexandria in November. His arrival was greeted with great anticipation. People from the city and the surrounding region streamed together just to catch a glimpse of him. Services of prayer and thanksgiving were held in all the churches. It was a time of great joy. His beloved clergy said that it was the happiest day of their lives. Finally after two years, their Bishop was home once again.

Despite the great celebration, not all things were peaceful. The Arians still had the sympathies of the Jews and pagans. They continued to foment opposition against Athanasius. Civil disturbances followed. Prefect Theodorus, however, was able to keep them in check. But the mouths of the Arians were not so easily silenced. Rumors were bandied about that the monks were on the side of the Arians. It was even said that the blessed hermit Antony favored the Arian cause. These accusations, coupled with the urgent invitation of the Church, brought Antony out of the desert. Leaving his quiet abode behind, the great ascetic journeyed to Alexandria. There he was joyfully received by his long-time friend Athanasius and by all the faithful.

The Arian bluff had been called. Antony wasted no time in denouncing Arianism. He said that their heresy was the forerunner of the Antichrist. He told the people that the Son of God was not a created being, but that He was the eternal Word and Wisdom of the Father. To say that "there was a time when He was not" was impious. Antony said that there could be no fellowship with the Arians, because there can be no communion between light and darkness.

The faithful were not alone in rejoicing at his coming. Antony's fame and magnetism attracted the whole city. Even pagans and their priests came to the church to see "the man of God." Many wanted just to touch him. Some who did received more than just a touch, for Antony was a miracle worker. He healed many demoniacs and the insane. His visit had a dramatic impact upon the city. In the few short days that he spent there, Athanasius said more people became Christians than normally would do so in an entire year. Rejoicing along with the people, Antony returned once again to his home in the desert.

But as Antony, the friend of God, was working for good, the enemies of God were working for evil. Against the conservative laity, who were by and large firmly dedicated to the orthodox truth, the Arians made few inroads, but against the clergy the Arians did better. By intrigue, stratagem, and coercion, a good many bishops were swayed. In time many of the major sees of the East came under Arian influence. This did not bode well for the future of the Church.

Meanwhile, Eusebius left his bishopric in Nicomedia to become the Patriarch at Constantinople. This move, though a controversial one at the time, was a favorable one for the Arians. Eusebius was now in the capital city of the Empire and he had the ear of Emperor Constantius. He did not waste any time in filling that ear. Athanasius, he said, had returned to his see in violation of the council of Tyre. Constantine II was wrong to restore him. The council had deposed him and only the council had the right to restore him. (Technically, Eusebius had a point, if one were to put any stock at all in the proceedings at Tyre.) Of course, the Eusebians had more to say as well. They accused the Patriarch of violence against the Alexandrian citizens. They also said that he had embezzled funds that had been set aside for the support of widows. In short, he was unfit to be Bishop and so they consecrated one of their own to replace him. Pistus, one of the Arian priests excommunicated at Nicea, was chosen. Their plan was to get rid of Athanasius once again and to install Pistus in his place.

In his Paschal Letter of 339 Athanasius expressed his feelings over this Arian treachery. "Let us make a joyful noise with the saints, and let not one of us fail of his duty in these things; counting as nothing the affliction of the trials which, especially at this time, have been enviously directed against us by the party of Eusebius. Even now they wish to injure us, and by their accusations to encompass our death.... But, as faithful servants of God, knowing that He is our salvation in the time of trouble, for our Lord promised us beforehand, saying, 'Blessed are you when men revile you and persecute you, and say all manner of evil against you falsely, for my sake. Rejoice and be exceedingly glad, for your reward is great in Heaven.'"[26]

To test the waters, the Arians sent a delegation to Rome. This delegation consisted of an Arian priest named Macarius and two deacons. The purpose of their delegation was to meet with Pope Julius. They intended to present allegations against Athanasius, with the hope that Julius would side with them to force the Patriarch out. Secondly, they planned to nominate Pistus to be his replacement. Athanasius learned of the delegation's departure and immediately summoned the Egyptian bishops to council. This was during the winter of 338-339. The synod of bishops drafted a letter in defense of Patriarch Athanasius. Two priests were quickly dispatched to carry the letter to Julius.

After both parties arrived at Rome, the irregularity of Pistus' consecration became evident. At this revelation, Macarius gave up and deserted his delegation. The Arian deacons, however, remained and requested that a council be called to judge the charges against Athanasius. This seemed reasonable to Julius and so he invited all the parties concerned to attend. But the council never took place. The Arians, realizing that there was no support for Pistus' nomination, declined to participate. Instead they assembled at Antioch (the winter residence of Constantius). There they consecrated a new nominee for Athanasius' see. They chose Gregory, a Cappadocian, who had been a former student at Alexandria.

Constantius added force to the Arian cause. He removed the prefect Theodorus from Alexandria and replaced him with Philagrius. The new prefect would not be so favorable to the Patriarch. Having been the prefect once before, he was already known to the Alexandrians as an apostate, a persecutor of the Church, and a man of ill character.

The stage was now set. The Arians were ready to strike. The blow came during Lent in March of 339 on a Sunday. Athanasius was at the Church of Theonas. Many baptisms had been held there that morning. A report came to him that soldiers under Philagrius were on their way to seize him. Athanasius immediately left the church before the soldiers arrived and disappeared into the city. He remained hidden within the walls of Alexandria. Four days passed. Then a military guard escorted Gregory into the city to assume the Bishop's place.

True to his character, Philagrius incited Jews and heathens against the faithful. Gregory served as his accomplice. A persecution ensued. Violent mobs armed with swords and clubs descended upon the churches of the city. Plunder and desecration followed. Heathen sacrifices were made on the altars. Lewd acts were committed. The reserved sacrament was consumed and trampled under foot. The clergy, monks, and laity were humiliated and beaten. Some were imprisoned. Others were killed. The Patriarch's own aunt was one of those who were murdered. Nuns were stripped, beaten, and even raped.

Following this initial onslaught, the persecution widened. Gregory insisted that everyone hold communion with him. Those who refused were beaten or scourged. In addition he confiscated the alms that had been collected for the support of the poor and widowed. This "bishop" of Satan also sent persecutors out into the countryside. At their hands, bishops were scourged and imprisoned. One of these, Bishop Potammon, who had lost an eye in the persecution of Diocletian, was so severely beaten that he died from his wounds. All this was done in the name of Arianism. For the next four weeks Athanasius remained hidden within the city. During this time he drafted an urgent appeal. It was sent out as a circular letter to bishops everywhere. After describing the events that had occurred, he urged all bishops to be of one accord in rejecting the Arian cause. He exhorted all of them to remain true to the faith. He also asked them to respond in writing to show their support. His hope was that the unanimity of their leadership would cause the Arians, and their supporters, to repent of their deeds and stop their violence.

After this Athanasius secretly left the city. Accompanied by a few of his clergy, he made his way to Rome. Within the next few months other exiles joined him there.

When Pachomius, the monastic leader of the desert, learned of these events he was deeply grieved. Saddened that the people of God had been so wronged and deprived of their Archbishop, he spoke to the monks, "We believe in the Lord. He has permitted this to happen in order to test the faithful, but punishment will come swiftly and will not tarry.... As for the most holy Pope Athanasius, against whom the enemies have been battling so long, he is most truly blessed. They have no power against him for he has God to sustain his faith."[27]

This exile was to be the longest for the persecuted Bishop. From April 339 to October 346 he was absent from his people. While at Rome his official duties were few, and so he busied himself in other ways. Much of his time was spent in prayer, both privately and at the services of the Church. The following winter, instead of his usual Paschal Letter, Athanasius sent a short note to his entrusted friend, Bishop Serapion, asking him to make the necessary announcements for Lent. At Alexandria the intruder Gregory made his own attempt to set the date for Holy Pascha. It was an amateurish attempt. Midway through Lent, it was discovered that he had made a mistake. His miscalculation had added an extra week to the austerities of Lent. His mistake was a cause for considerable ridicule by the populace.

The years of exile that followed were marked by a series of councils on both sides. The Arians and their sympathizers made efforts to draft a new creed that could be accepted as being true to the apostolic tradition without being so. The supporters of Athanasius attempted to clear the name of the Patriarch and to have him restored. In the spring of 340 a delegation from the Arians came to Rome. They brought with them a letter stating their case against the Patriarch. Pope Julius had hoped that bishops from the East would come as well, so that a council could be held. But when none came, he convened a council of Italian bishops instead. They examined the charges against Athanasius and the charges that had been brought against the other exiles as well. They had no trouble in exonerating the Patriarch of all charges. The exiles with him were also pronounced innocent. (Julius' help was of great importance to Athanasius. His aid echoed far beyond the walls of the ancient city. As the Bishop of Rome, his actions had great influence upon all the churches of the West. His support brought with it the support of many others as well.)

After the council Julius drafted a letter to the eastern bishops informing them of their decision. He admonished the Arians for the letter that they had previously sent to him. Pointing out their pride and arrogance, Julius stated that "in ecclesiastical matters, it is not a display of eloquence that is needed, but the observance of the Apostolic Canons, and an earnest care not to offend one of the little ones of the Church."²⁸ The letter was sent to the eastern bishops who were gathered in council at Antioch. (At this eastern council four different creeds were proposed in an attempt to circumvent the faith of Nicea. None of the creeds gained any notable following. None deserved any.)

Meanwhile, Julius, foreseeing no conclusion to the matter, referred the dispute to Caesar Constans for his consideration. (Constans was an admirer of Athanasius. Previously, the Bishop had sent a letter of defense to him. When Constans wrote back, Athanasius then sent him a bound copy of the Scriptures as a gift.) Constans asked his brother Constantius to send a delegation of bishops from the East to state their case against Athanasius. A few bishops, who had attended the dedication of the Church of the Holy Sepulcher, reassembled in the winter of 341 to appoint representatives for this council.

Amid the trouble and anguish of exile, Athanasius sent a Paschal Letter of encouragement to his people: "The gladness of our Feast, my brethren, is always near at hand, and never fails those who wish to celebrate it. For the Word is near, Who is all things on our behalf, even our Lord Jesus Christ, Who having promised that His habitation with us should be perpetual, in virtue of that cried, saying, 'Lo, I am with you all the days of the world.' [cf. Mt 28:20] For as He is the Shepherd, and the High Priest, and the Way and the Door, and everything at once to us, so again He has shown to us this Feast and Holy Day."²⁹

In the summer of 342 the delegation from the eastern bishops arrived at Treveri to present their case to Constans. Heeding the warnings of Bishop Maximinus not to accept their arguments, Constans sent the Arians away in disgrace. Constans then concluded that a general council was needed to bring an end to the controversy. He wrote Constantius of his desire. Constans informed Athanasius of his intentions and summoned him to Treveri. Upon his arrival, Athanasius met with the venerable Bishop Hosius and other clergy. There he learned that the Emperors had agreed to hold a council at Sardica. The Patriarch spent the Easter of 343 at Treveri.

The council at Sardica was convened in the summer. Proceedings were delayed while the bishops debated whether Athanasius should be allowed to attend. The Arians, of course, were opposed. The majority of the bishops, however, voted in favor of it. That night in reaction to the decision the Arians promptly left the city. On their way home they wrote a wild and angry protest, condemning everyone at the council, especially Athanasius, Julius, and Hosius. They distributed this document far and wide.

The rest of the bishops at the council carried on without the Arians. They carefully examined the charges against Athanasius and his fellow exiles. Finding no fault, they dismissed the charges. An encyclical letter of their decision was sent out to all the churches. The letter condemned the Arian leaders, branding them as wolves, who had invaded the Church. A separate letter was sent specifically to Alexandria and the Church of Egypt. In addition, Julius wrote a personal letter to the Alexandrians, saying, "I also congratulate no less my brother Athanasius, in that, though he is enduring many afflictions, he has at no time been forgetful of your love and earnest desires toward him. For although for a season he seemed to be withdrawn from you in body, yet he has continued to live always present with you in spirit."[30]

The result of the council was not peaceful. Constantius joined in the consternation of the Arians. He began a persecution in his realm against those of the Nicene faith. At Hadrianople savage cruelties were committed. Ten people were beheaded. At Trajanople, Bishop Theodulus was severely beaten and later died from his injuries. In Egypt there was also continued trouble for the Church.

However, one of the men who was responsible for the persecution quickly received his due reward. Balacius, a commander of the military in Egypt, zealously afflicted the Christians. Saint Antony of the desert was deeply disturbed by this and sent a letter of warning to the commander. He said that if Balacius did not stop his attacks, he would face the wrath of God. Balacius had nothing but contempt for the letter. He threatened to search out Antony and persecute him as well. Five days passed. Then as Balacius was riding on horseback, a companion's horse went berserk and viciously attacked him. He died three days later.

In the meantime Constantius made plans to capture Athanasius should he attempt to return to Alexandria. A watch was placed at all the ports and gates of the city. The magistrates were given strict orders: if the Bishop attempted to enter the city, he was to be executed. Athanasius, however, remained in exile. He spent the winter of 344 at Naissus.

Meanwhile, Constans was working to aid Athanasius' return. He sent Bishop Vincentius of Capus and Bishop Euphrates of Agrippina to Antioch to meet with Constantius. They were to impress upon him the urgent need for the Patriarch's restoration. It was hinted that if Constantius resisted, it would be regarded as a cause of war. Constans' efforts were given an unexpected boost from an unlikely source. A trick by the Arians backfired.

The Arian bishop Stephen sought to discredit Bishop Euphrates. He concocted a treacherous scheme. He hired a prostitute and had her enter Euphrates' bedroom at night in an attempt to seduce him. However, when the prostitute realized that the man she was sent to seduce was an elderly bishop, she balked. The plot then became public. After this debacle, Stephen was deposed and Constantius changed course. In August of 344 he ended the persecution and restored some of those who had been exiled from Egypt.

Athanasius spent the Easter of 345 at Aquileia with Constans. The following June the Arian impostor Gregory died in Alexandria. (He had been in bad health for four years.) Constantius then wrote to Athanasius requesting that he meet with him to discuss his possible restoration. Athanasius was wary and did not go.

About this time Pachomius confided to his monks concerning Athanasius: "In Egypt now in our generation, I see three principal things flourishing with the favor of God and man. The first is the blessed athlete, the holy Apa Athanasius, the archbishop of Alexandria who struggles for the faith even to the point of death."[31]

Athanasius then received two more letters from Constantius requesting a meeting. Finally, he acquiesced. Committing the whole matter to God, he began his journey. He passed through Rome and bid farewell to his faithful friend, Bishop Julius. Then proceeding to Trier, he thanked Constans for his invaluable support. He then traveled by way of Hadrianople to Antioch. There he was received by Constantius. The outcome of their meeting was favorable. Constantius restored him to his see and gave him assurances of good will in the future.

Athanasius now headed for home. At Jerusalem he was welcomed by a council which Bishop Maximus had convened. The council addressed a letter to the Church of Egypt: "We cannot give worthy thanks to the God of all, dearly beloved, for the wonderful things which He has done at all times, and especially at this time for your Church, in restoring to you your pastor and lord, and our fellow-minister Athanasius. For who ever hoped that his eyes would see what you are now actually obtaining? Of a truth, your prayers have been heard by the God of all, Who cares for His Church, and has looked upon your tears and groans, and has therefore heard your petitions."[32]

As Athanasius journeyed along the way, those, who were friendly, met him with rejoicing. Those, who were not, were afraid to show their faces. Others, who had written against him, repented of their actions, some confessing that they had written under compulsion. Finally in October of 346 Athanasius arrived in his beloved homeland. People came out from as far as a hundred miles distant from Alexandria to greet him. At Alexandria he was welcomed amidst great rejoicing by the clergy and all the faithful. He had been gone seven years.

CHAPTER SEVEN

PASTOR AND TEACHER

"Shepherd the flock of God which is among you, serving as
overseers, not by constraint but willingly, not for dishonest gain
but eagerly; nor as being lords over those entrusted to you, but
being examples to the flock; and when the Chief Shepherd appears,
you will receive the crown of glory that does not fade away."

1 Peter 5:2-4

Athanasius' heart was full of thanksgiving and joy upon returning to Alexandria. To once again be with the people whom he so
dearly loved was a great blessing. He had been gone many years.
But though he had been separated from his beloved flock and
homeland, he had always remained faithful to them. In exile his
love and care for his people had not waned. For even though he
could not be with them in body, he had remained with them in
spirit. During this time his communication with them had been
primarily through letters. These letters, entrusted to loyal and se-
cretive couriers, were the only way he could keep in contact. It
was the best that he could do at the time. But now he was home.
He was with his people. He could communicate with them, embrace them, encourage them, and love them in person.

The Patriarch's first Paschal Letter to be written from home
in seven years was especially dear to him. He gave praise to God

for bringing him home from afar: "Blessed is God, the Father of our Lord Jesus Christ, for such an introduction is fitting for an epistle, and more especially now, when it brings thanksgiving to the Lord, in the Apostle's words, because He has brought us from a distance, and granted us again to send openly to you, as usual, the Festal Letters."[33] Athanasius gave his usual encouraging words and instructions for the holy season of Lent and Easter. But thanksgiving was at the center of his letter: "Therefore let us, my brethren, looking forward to celebrate the eternal joy in heaven, keep the feast here also, rejoicing at all times, praying incessantly, and in everything giving thanks to the Lord. I give thanks to God, and for the various helps that have now been granted to us, in that though He has chastened us sorely, He did not deliver us over to death, but brought us from a distance, even as from the ends of the earth, and has united us again with you."[34]

All the faithful of Egypt rejoiced at Athanasius' return. Both the clergy and the people were filled with inexpressible delight. Almost contrary to hope, they had received back their true shepherd and master. Many beyond the realm of Egypt rejoiced as well. Upon his return the Patriarch received over four hundred letters from all parts of the Empire. Most offered congratulations, along with thanksgivings to God. Others requested forgiveness for having sided with the Arians under duress.

While Athanasius was in exile, the Christians of Alexandria and Egypt had remained steadfast in their faith. Even without their beloved leader they carried on. Under persecution from the Arian mob and their cohorts they persevered. The times required that the faithful pull inward for survival. Their corporate Christian life was put on hold in many ways. It was as if a season of spiritual winter had enveloped the Church — a time of waiting, but with the hope and anticipation of a spiritual spring yet to come. With the arrival of their beloved Bishop back in Egypt, this waiting came to an end. Hope was fulfilled. And with their spiritual head now present, a reawakening of the Church in Egypt took place.

This reawakening spread like a spiritual fire, and the results were divine. The faithful greatly encouraged one another towards greater virtue. Parents encouraged their children toward holiness, and children encouraged their parents. Spouses persuaded one another to spend time in prayer. Good works abounded. Many widows and orphans, who went hungry and unclothed during the reign of the Arians, now received the necessary care which they so desperately needed. Indeed, so great was the zeal of the faithful, wrote Athanasius, "that you would have thought every family and every house to be a church, by the reason of the goodness of its members, and the prayers which were offered to God."[35]

During this time many embraced the monastic life. A good number of young women, who had previously contemplated marriage, instead decided to remain virgins to Christ. Young men, too, received the monastic habit. One of these was a young man named Ammon, who was afterwards to become a bishop. Later in life he recalled that at the age of seventeen: "I heard the blessed Pope Athanasius relating in church the way of life of the monks and ever-virgins and marveling at the hope stored up for them in the heavens. Loving what I had heard from him, I went out and chose their blessed way of life for myself."[36]

The call to holiness was not limited to just monastics. Athanasius entreated all the faithful to live a holy life. Christians everywhere were encouraged to cut themselves off from worldly desires and to avoid gluttony, dishonesty, drunkenness, and excessive leisure. Indeed, some of the laity even rivaled the monastics in their ascetic labors. Those that did, Athanasius said, practice discipline in the life of the angels, die daily, and crucify their passions. "Vegetables replace meats for such people, and water replaces wine, sparse meals replace abundant meals. Moreover, for this reason, they keep vigils rather than sleep, and nights of prayer to God often replace daytime for them, along with meditation on His law and blessings."[37]

The growth of the Church can be seen from an incident which occurred at Lent during this period. So great were the crowds that came for worship during this holy season that the churches could scarcely contain them. During the services people were tightly packed together. The overcrowding caused suffering, especially with the children and the elderly. Some fainted from the heat and had to be carried to their homes afterward. This overcrowding led to a clamor for the use of the Church of the Caesareum (a large but as yet uncompleted edifice). Athanasius relented. Easter services were held in the unfinished church even though it had not yet been dedicated. (The Arians later denounced Athanasius for making this decision, but he responded to Emperor Constantius, saying, "You, at least, I am sure, as a lover of God will approve of the people's zeal, and will pardon me for being unwilling to hinder the prayers of so great a multitude."[38]) Supported by this outpouring of piety, Athanasius worked diligently to strengthen the Church. As Patriarch, he had the responsibility for all the churches throughout Egypt and Libya. All the bishops of these regions were under his authority. It was his duty not only to work with these bishops in governing and administering the affairs of the Church, but also to appoint new bishops as vacancies to the episcopate arose. Athanasius astutely chose the best candidates to fill these positions. The men chosen were always devout followers of God and true adherents to Nicene Christology. Many of them were monks. Thus, as the years of peace in Egypt increased, so did the unanimity of the bishops increase. Left in peace, the Church increased in peace.

However, all was not so peaceful outside of Egypt. Though not able to prevent his return to Egypt, the enemies of Athanasius were far from giving up. They continued to pursue their efforts against the Patriarch at a time when he seemed untouchable. Athanasius had strong support within Egypt and an ally in Caesar Constans, who was an effective counterbalance to his Arianizing brother Constantius. But this delicate balance of power changed abruptly in the year 350 when Constans was murdered. Had Constantius been free of troubles, he might have once again pursued Athanasius at this point. However, his ascension to the position of sole Emperor did not go uncontested. There were rivals to deal with, the chief of these being Magnentius. It was not until 353 that Constantius was able to finally suppress the threats against his throne.

Athanasius, in the meantime, saw trouble on the horizon. He suspected that a revival of charges against him might be forthcoming. In anticipation of this in about 351 he wrote his *Defense Against the Arians*. In this book Athanasius reiterated the charges that had been brought against him by the Arians, as well as the decisions that had been rendered in his favor by the various councils and leaders of the Church. The actual documents and letters of these groups were included in his work as proof of his statements. His personal testimony to the events which occurred, along with his accuracy of reporting and his use of original documents, made the *Defense* the most reliable source of history for this period.

By the year 353 the sole rule of Constantius had begun to inspire Athanasius' enemies. In hope of heading off trouble, the

Patriarch sent a delegation, led by his trusted assistant, Bishop Serapion, to speak with Constantius, who was then at Milan. Not long after the delegation's departure, Montanus, an officer of the Imperial Court, arrived in Alexandria with a letter for the Patriarch. The letter stated that no delegation would be received by the Emperor, but that Athanasius' request for a personal audience had been granted. Since he had not requested any such audience, Athanasius became suspicious. The letter did not actually command him to go to Italy, so he did not. Instead, he simply conveyed his willingness to do so if ordered.

By the year 355 matters had come to a head. Diogenes, the Secretary of the Emperor, arrived in Alexandria with the intention of seizing Bishop Athanasius. Between September and December several attempts were made to capture him. Diogenes and his forces actually stormed one of the churches in an attempt to arrest him, but the people formed a human shield around the Patriarch and vehemently resisted all efforts to seize him. The pressure, however, continued to mount. In January of 356 Duke Syrianus arrived in Alexandria. He began to gather a large army. Soldiers from the legions stationed throughout Egypt and Libya were brought into the city. His actions provided much cause for rumor. Athanasius inquired of the Duke as to whether he had orders from the Court. Syrianus replied that he did not.

The ensuing calm lasted but a month. At midnight on February 8, as Athanasius was attending the Vigil Service in the Church of Theonas, the soldiers of Syrianus suddenly surrounded the church. During the commotion the Bishop was seated on his throne and he instructed the deacon to begin the chanting of Psalm 136. Suddenly, the troops, armed with swords, bows, spears, and clubs, burst through the church doors. Pandemonium ensued.

Swords flashed. People were trampled under foot as they rushed to escape. The Bishop's intent was to remain in the church until the faithful had made their way out. But as the soldiers pushed forward towards the front of the church to capture Athanasius, the clergy and monks surrounded their beloved Patriarch. In the confusion that followed they managed to spirit him out of the church to safety. He disappeared into the night. His escape had been nothing short of miraculous.

CHAPTER EIGHT

THE DESERT

"The wilderness and the wasteland shall be glad for them, and the
desert shall rejoice and blossom as the rose; it shall blossom
abundantly and rejoice, even with joy and singing..."

Isaiah 35:1-2

Athanasius had eluded the grasp of Duke Syrianus. Though his
troops scoured the city for the Patriarch, he was nowhere to be
found. The great city of Alexandria could provide many a hiding
place. The soldiers searched everywhere, but it was a fruitless effort for the Bishop was not to be found in the city. He had already left. After escaping the Church of Theonas, the monks had
escorted him out of town. He was now safe in the monastic cells
of the nearby Nitrian desert.

The Patriarch always had a special place in his heart for the
monks. The esteem was mutual. Athanasius was one of them. He
was both their father and their brother. The desert was also his
home. Among these faithful friends and followers he would make
his refuge. During this trial the Patriarch's expressed attitude was
that of the Psalmist: "The Lord is my light and my salvation;
whom shall I fear? The Lord is the strength of my life; of whom
shall I be afraid?" (Ps. 27:1)

When Athanasius was not found in the city, Syrianus expanded the search. The towns, villages, and monasteries of the desert were searched. All was in vain, however. Though many were interrogated, not a single clue was found as to the Bishop's whereabouts. Some, of course, knew quite well where he was, but no one betrayed him.

Though he had been sought out by the Duke, Athanasius did not believe that the Emperor Constantius was behind the persecution. He did not feel that the Emperor would go back on the assurances that he had received from him at Antioch when he was returning from exile. So he decided to take his case directly to Constantius himself. His plan was to cross the Libyan desert and then to sail for Italy. His hope was to meet with Constantius in Milan. When preparations were complete, Athanasius set out on his journey with a handful of faithful clergy. But along the way he received disturbing news. There were reports of the widespread banishment of bishops, who had refused to join in his condemnation. In Egypt sixteen bishops had been banished, and there was word of violence in Alexandria. Despite these reports, the Patriarch continued on his journey, still hoping to meet with the Emperor.

When Athanasius arrived in Libya, he received copies of two letters that had been sent out by the Emperor. In the first letter Constantius viciously denounced the Patriarch: "That pestilent fellow Athanasius is driven from place to place, for which he would only suffer the punishment he deserves, if one were to kill him ten times over."[39] The letter also called for a certain George to take his place as bishop. The second letter was directed toward Bishop Frumentius of Auxumis, who had been consecrated by Athanasius. Frumentius was summoned so that he might be taught by the "venerable George," in order to unlearn what he had been taught by "the most wicked Athanasius… a man who is guilty of ten thousand crimes."[40] Upon learning of this, Athanasius now realized that Constantius himself was behind the persecution. An appeal to him was out of the question.

The Patriarch decided that his best course of action was to return to the Egyptian desert. Before setting out, he drafted a letter to the bishops of Egypt. It was composed about Easter of 356. In his letter he warned the bishops about the Arian heretics. These false prophets, he said, "deck themselves out in the language of Scripture, speaking indeed the words, but stealing away the true meaning; and so disguising by tricks their false inventions, they also become murderers of those whom they have led astray." Their heresy, he said, is like a gangrene, which eats its way everywhere. "Resist them as apostates" he continued and endure to the end, keeping the faith, that you might receive the crown of glory, which God has promised to those who love Him.[41]

Meanwhile there was trouble in Alexandria. On Holy Pascha the faithful had gathered at the cemetery to remember the departed and to celebrate the resurrection when Duke Syrianus' troops showed up. They had not come to join in worship. Without provocation, they attacked the faithful, who were guilty of nothing but prayer. The troops used violence to disperse the crowd. Neither women nor children were spared. The holy virgins were even stripped and humiliated. In the ensuing violence some of the faithful were murdered.

In June the new governor Cataphronius arrived, accompanied by Count Heraclius. They brought with them a letter from Constantius, which was addressed to the pagans of the area. They were directed to aid in the Arian persecution of Athanasius' followers. If they failed to do so, they were threatened with severe punishment. Many of them had no animosity against the Church, and they followed this order with reluctance. Heraclius also announced an imperial decree that all the churches were to be turned over to the Arians. In addition, all magistrates were to sign a written statement, agreeing to carry out the persecution and to accept George as the Emperor's new choice for bishop.

The next attack came when most of the faithful had departed from the Church of the Theonas following an all-night vigil. Some women who had remained behind were murdered. The church was wrecked and polluted with heathen orgies. The violence then spilled over into the city. On the pretense of "looking for Athanasius," houses were ransacked and tombs desecrated. The military commander Sebastian zealously oversaw the carrying out of these atrocities.

Following this, the persecution spread into the countryside. Houses were plundered. Monasteries were overthrown. Monks were attacked. Widows were insulted and denied aid. Clergy and nuns were beaten. Bishops were banished or forced into labor in the mines. In June the churches of Alexandria were turned over to the Arians. The Arian replacements for the clergy, who had been banished, were a motley crew that included dissolute youths, bigamists, and those chosen because of their wealth or power.

During Lent of the following year in 357 George was installed as the new "bishop" of the city. His qualifications for the office were straightforward. He had none. George had been a pork-contractor in Constantinople and, according to some, a dishonest one. He had accumulated considerable wealth and was an ardent Arian. His violent temper, perhaps, recommended him to the Arians as one who could be counted upon to deal harshly with the Church. He arrived at his post with an armed guard and soon picked up where others had left off in persecuting the faithful. (There was an uncanny similarity between George and Gregory, an earlier impostor at Alexandria. Both were from Cappadocia.

Both were Arians. Both arrived during Lent with an armed guard. Both used similar violence and force against the Church.)

In the week after Pentecost George ordered the commander Sebastian into action. A number of the faithful who were worshipping in the cemetery, rather than communicate with the Arians, were attacked. Many were killed and others from their number banished. In addition, the clergy continued to be persecuted. More of them were banished. Their families were even dragged out of their houses and beaten. Widows, too, were also subject to beatings. Besides violence, the Arians also employed deceit in their attack against the Church. They offered protection and bribes to anyone who would embrace Arianism. They also turned the justice system upside down. People were arrested and brought before the court, not for crimes committed, but for acts of kindness. Anyone who showed mercy to others was to be accused. Anyone who received mercy was to be beaten. It seems that the chief justice of the Arians was none other than the Devil himself.

Meanwhile Athanasius continued to elude those who sought him. From the desert he wrote his customary Paschal Letter. In it he encouraged the faithful in the midst of persecution. "For [God] did not permit the affliction to happen because He hates us, and He has not abandoned us because the lawless people are too strong; rather, He cares for us through the things that happen. Therefore, take courage: 'God has not abandoned His people whom He knew beforehand.'" (Rom 11:2)[42]

During this period the Patriarch changed his place of hiding from time to time. To avoid detection he did not remain in one location. Rather, he sought refuge in a variety of places throughout Egypt. He even spent part of the time within Alexandria itself. Once he hid in the home of one of the young virgins of the city. (Years later the monk Palladius met this virgin who was by then in her seventies. She related to him that she had been startled when the Bishop came to her house, but he assured her, by saying, "Just this night now God made it clear to me that I will be saved by no one but you."[43]) Most of this period of exile, however, was spent by Athanasius in the monastic cells of Upper and Lower Egypt. There among the faithful and loyal monks, he was in perfect safety. The monks were his trusted soldiers. They warned him of danger, informed him of news, and distributed his letters and writings.

Athanasius' flight into exile had not simply been one of reaction. He had carefully thought out the proper response to persecution. He wrote: "To all men generally, even to us, this law is given, to flee when persecuted, and to hide when sought after, and not rashly tempt the Lord, ...but that men should be ready, that, when the time comes, or when they are taken, they may contend for the truth even unto death. This rule the blessed martyrs observed in their several persecutions. When persecuted they fled, while concealing themselves they showed fortitude, and when discovered they submitted to martyrdom."[44]

With Athanasius driven out, the authorities mistakenly assumed that they had the upper hand. The Patriarch was gone. George had taken his place. And they had an army. But they neglected to consider the old maxim that "the pen is mightier than the sword." During his exile Athanasius used his pen as a powerful weapon. In fact, this exile from 356 to 362 was the most prolific period of writing in his life. His authorship from the desert include two important books on the Arians: the *History of the Arians* and the *Four Discourses Against the Arians*. As important as these works were, especially in relation to the times, another work had greater impact. It was the biography of Saint Antony, the father of monks, entitled the *Life of Antony*. Had Athanasius not done anything else in his life, he would have been famous for writing this one book alone. During his lifetime it was the most influential of all his works.

The *Life of Antony* was a "best seller" of its day. It was quickly translated from Greek into Latin and gained wide circulation in both the East and the West. The book had an appeal to many different kinds of people. It was of interest both to the Christian and to the non-Christian, to the wise man and to the common man, to the married and to the celibate. As a personal friend, Athanasius knew Antony well. In his book he chronicled Antony's solitude (twenty years alone in a cave), his prayer, his fasting, his simple dress, his labor of weaving, and his disregard for comfort or pleasure. Antony passed the night without sleep. He ate only bread and salt once a day. He prophesied events, performed miracles, and struggled against the demons. His fame brought many to seek out his advice.

In the desert, through asceticism and with the help of God, Antony's soul was purified. He grew close to God — to the point where he could say, "I no longer fear God, I love Him." Thus, the desert became for him, not so much an escape from the world, but a holy temple from which he offered up prayers to God for all mankind. His struggles were not against the seen, but against the unseen. His life revealed a new kind of martyrdom — a bloodless martyrdom. It was not the martyrdom of an instant, but the martyrdom of a lifetime of self-sacrifice and devotion to God.

The impact of Athanasius' biography of Antony was widespread. It made a keen impression on all those who read or heard of it. Many of the early Fathers of the Church were familiar with it. Christians from all walks of life were encouraged by it. Others became Christians because of it. Gregory of Nazianzus called it a monastic rule in a narrative form. As a result of this, many, even from the ranks of the military and the wealthy, flocked to the desert in imitation of Antony (so much so that Athanasius said the desert hills were filled with divine music).

Antony's way of life was that of the solitary and his devotion to God became an example for all monks. However, it was cenobitic, or communal, monasticism, as fostered by Pachomius, that was to become the norm for those seeking the ascetic life. Nonetheless, all the monks still looked to Antony as their common father. Antony remained the most famous of all the desert dwellers. And it was the pen of Athanasius' exile that made him so well known.

Meanwhile George continued to persecute the Church of Egypt. Soldiers not only banished the clergy, but also went out into the desert and laid their hands on the hermits. The pressure was too much for Theodore, the Bishop of Oxyrynchus in middle Egypt. He caved in and submitted himself to George's authority. George then forced him to be reordained. Upon hearing of Theodore's lapse, the faithful of Oxyrynchus refused to have anything to do with him, and carried on without him. In all this their attitude toward the Arians was certainly that of their beloved Patriarch. "For what is there that the Arians leave undone? They watch the roads, observe those who enter and leave the city, search the vessels, go around the deserts, ransack houses, harass the brethren, cause unrest to everybody."[45]

Athanasius agonized over the persecution that had come upon God's faithful people. He asked others to pray that God would deliver the Church from persecution. It was his desire that those who had fallen away might be raised up from the pit of falsehood and return to the true faith. For he said that they were like "wandering, poor people." He was also grieved at not being able to be with his faithful followers. "For my eyes ceased not from tears, nor my spirit from groaning, because we are not permitted even to see the brethren. But God is my witness, that on account of their persecution I have not been able to see even my parents whom I have."[46]

George was not content to simply persecute the Church. In 358 he began violent measures against the pagans and their worship services as well. However, he soon regretted this decision. The pagans were not used to turning the other cheek. In response to George's attack, they returned violence for violence. An angry mob gathered and descended upon George in an attempt to kill him. George was rescued by the authorities with difficulty. Realizing the danger that he was in, he quickly fled the city. With George gone, the followers of Athanasius were then able to retake control of the churches. But this turn of events lasted only two months. When Commander Sebastian returned from the desert with his forces, he turned the churches back over to the Arians. He evicted the faithful with violence and bloodshed.

Throughout all this Athanasius' hope and prayer was that "the guilty and murderous heresy of the Arians may disappear, and the truth may shine again in the hearts of all. So that all everywhere may say the same thing and think the same thing, and that, no Arian insolence remaining, it may be said and confessed in every church, 'one Lord, one faith, one baptism.'" (Eph 4:5)[47]

George was in no hurry to return to Egypt. He remained away for over two years. But in November of 361 he grew bolder and decided to return to his former rule. This turned out to be a mistake. His new rule was short. Four days after he arrived, he was seized by a mob and imprisoned. A month later on Christmas Eve he was dragged out of prison by the pagans and hanged.

About this same time, Emperor Constantius became ill and

died. Upon his death Julian became the new Emperor. One of his first edicts was issued in February of 362. The edict called for the return of all those who had been exiled by Constantius. All exiles were free to return home. After six years Athanasius' third exile was now over. He could return once again to Alexandria and to his beloved faithful.

CHAPTER NINE

THE LAST YEARS

"...I see the heavens opened and the Son of Man
standing at the right hand of God!"

Acts 7:56

Athanasius was to have only eight months of peace, but they were
eight months well spent. One of his first acts was to convene a
synod of bishops at Alexandria. It was a gathering of saints and
confessors. Many of those who attended were bishops who had
suffered under the wicked George. Though the number of attend-
ees at the synod was not great, the impact of their decision was.

The purpose of the council was to address the issue of those
who had wandered from the true faith and strayed into Arianism.
There were people who had joined the Arian heresy out of conviction. Others had done so out of fear of persecution. Some had
simply been deceived. Afterwards, when many of these came to
their senses and saw the error of their ways, they asked to return
to the Church. The question that the council had to answer was
just how these people should be received back. How was the
Church to deal with them?

The council's decision was to use mercy. Harsh measures
could have been justified. But Athanasius knew all too well the

wounds that had been inflicted upon these lost sheep and the medicine that was needed to heal them. His leadership set the tone. The bishops decided that those who desired to return to the Church should be received as parents would receive their wayward children. All those who earnestly desired to return to the true faith would be welcomed. The returnees were required only to anathematize the Arian heresy and to confess the true faith of Nicea. This same pattern was adopted by other churches throughout the Empire. Saint Jerome, in later writing about this decision, stated that this conciliatory approach "snatched the world from the jaws of Satan," avoided countless schisms, and kept many in the Church who might otherwise have been driven back into Arianism.[48]

Not long after this, the new Emperor Julian began to show his true colors. Julian was the son of the half-brother of Constantine. He had received Christian instruction under Eusebius of Nicomedia. After he was baptized, he began training for the priesthood. However, after studying Greek and pagan philosophy at Athens, he gave himself over to paganism, but he kept this a secret. When he became Emperor he revealed his secret. He let it be known that he no longer believed in Christianity. He now confessed that he believed in the ancient Roman gods. (From this time on he was known as Julian the Apostate.) His stated goal as Emperor was to rule under the principles of paganism.

Regarding the exiles, Julian now clarified his intent. He stated that he had wanted the exiles only to return to their homes, not to their ecclesiastical duties. Concerning Athanasius in particular, he said that the Patriarch should have asked special permission to return to Alexandria since he had received so many sentences in the past. Now he declared that Athanasius must leave Alexandria at once or face severe punishment. All of the faithful were sorely distressed by this. An urgent appeal was made. The

Emperor was asked to reconsider. An indignant response came back. The prefect Ecdikius Olympus was threatened with a heavy fine if Athanasius, "the enemy of the gods," did not leave Alexandria at once. The Bishop had no choice. Preparations were made for his departure. As he was leaving, Athanasius consoled his followers by saying, "It is only a cloud, and will soon pass away."[49] Then Athanasius and a few companions departed the city.

After leaving Alexandria, the Bishop and his party headed by boat up the Nile River toward Upper Egypt. But they were not alone in their journey for long. Government forces were soon on their trail. Apparently, the authorities had decided that they did not just want Athanasius out of Alexandria, they wanted him arrested and taken out of Egypt altogether. Athanasius' party soon realized that they were being followed. After awhile it became apparent that their pursuers were making better time on the river than they were. The pursuers were gaining on them. It seemed it would only be a matter of time before they would be overtaken. At this realization, Athanasius acted. He ordered the steersman to turn the boat around and head downstream — in the direction of the pursuers. The Bishop's command elicited astonishment. But with raised eyebrows and considerable apprehension, the order was followed. The boat was turned downstream. Gradually, the patrol boat came into clearer view. Closer and closer they came. Now within earshot. Then the authorities hollered out. They wanted to know if their party had seen Bishop Athanasius on the river. Athanasius' crew shouted back, "He is not far off." The authorities then thanked them and headed on upriver. They were completely fooled.

Athanasius' party continued downstream and returned to Chaereu, the first station on the road east of Alexandria. There they remained until the immediate danger of pursuit had passed.

Then they continued once again up the Nile. They journeyed to Upper Egypt as far as Upper Hermupolis in the Thebaid. It was Lent by the time they reached Hermupolis. A crowd awaited them. Lined on the banks of the river were about a hundred clergy and monks. Athanasius stepped ashore. He was then mounted on a donkey and led to the monastery. The monks led the way with the chanting of psalms.

While they were on their way to the monastery Abba Theodore arrived. He had been sent by Abba Horsiesios to greet the Patriarch on behalf of the monks near Seneset. Athanasius embraced Theodore and inquired about the brethren. "By the help of God and your holy prayers, we are all well," was his reply. When Theodore took the bridle of the Bishop's donkey to lead it, Athanasius protested. But Theodore explained, "Allow me, holy father, for is it not a favor for us to humble ourselves to the one who has often died for us for the sake of maintaining the faith of Christ." As they continued on, the Patriarch commented to those around him on the virtue of humility. "Are we worthy to say of ourselves, 'We are the fathers of the world'? Not really! Truly our fathers are these who have humility and submission to God. Truly happy and blessed are those who bear the cross at all times, whose greatness is due to their humility, and who will have rest after their labors, when they receive the imperishable crown."[50] When they arrived at the church of Smoun, Athanasius prayed for all the people gathered there.

A few days later the Patriarch and those with him went to visit the monasteries of Nouoi and Kahior. There he entered the church and prayed, and then visited the refectory and the monks' cells. Observing their buildings and way of life, Athanasius praised God and said to Theodore, "You have indeed established in the world something great and splendid which gives rest to every soul who comes to you." Theodore acknowledged the importance of the Patriarch's prayers for them, and added, "The Lord knows that when we saw Your Holiness, it was as if we had seen our Lord Jesus Christ in the heavenly Jerusalem, because of our great trust in you, for you are our father." When it came time to leave, the two embraced, Theodore received the Bishop's blessing, and Athanasius gave him a letter to deliver to Abba Horsiesios. As they departed Theodore said to him, "Our lord and father, remember us in your holy prayers."[51] To which the Patriarch replied "If I forget you, O Jerusalem, let my right hand be forgotten, yes, let my tongue cleave to the to the roof of my mouth, if I do not remember you."[52]

During midsummer of 363 Athanasius was near Antinoupolis. There he learned that the authorities were on his trail once again. Abba Theodore brought his covered boat to carry the Bishop up to Tabenne. Abba Pammon and others were with them. The monks towed the boat from shore with difficulty. Progress was slow as both the wind and the current were against them. Athanasius was concerned about their progress and prayed earnestly. Pammon spoke an encouraging word. Athanasius replied, "Believe me when I say that my heart is never so trustful in time of peace as in time of persecution. For I have good confidence that suffering for Christ, and strengthened by his mercy, even though I am slain, I shall find mercy with him." While he was still speaking, Theodore looked at Pammon and smiled. Pammon nearly laughed. Athanasius said, "Why have you laughed at my words? Do you convict me of cowardice?" Theodore said to Pammon, "Tell him why we smiled." Pammon replied, "You ought to tell him." So Theodore said, "In this very hour Julian has been slain in Persia." He then quickly added that the new Emperor would be a Christian and that Athanasius should soon go to meet him.[53]

Athanasius trusted the divine insight of these two holy elders. He took their words to heart and immediately reversed course and set off for Alexandria. He entered the city quietly and gathered a group of his trusted clergy. Together they set off on their journey with haste to meet with the new Emperor Jovian. They had reason to hurry. For the Arians were also on their way to meet Jovian. Athanasius traveled by way of Hierapolis to Edessa. There he met the Emperor and together they traveled to Antioch. At Antioch Jovian gave the Bishop an imperial letter granting him permission to return to his see: "To the most religious and friend of God, Athanasius. Admiring exceedingly the achievements of your most honorable life, and of your likeness to the God of all, and of your affection toward our Savior Christ, we accept you most honored bishop. And inasmuch as you have not flinched from all labor, nor from fear of your persecutors, and, regarding dangers and threats as dung, holding the rudder of the Orthodox faith which is dear to you, are contending even until now for the truth, and continue to exhibit yourself as a pattern to all the people of the faithful, and as an example of virtue: our imperial Majesty recalls you, and desires that you should return to the office of the teaching of salvation. Return then to the holy churches, and tend the people of God, and send up to God with zeal your prayers for our clemency."[54]

The Arians arrived after this. Having submitted their usual litany of complaints, they asked that Lucius, who had accompanied them, be named bishop in Athanasius' place. Jovian replied that the matter had already been settled and that Athanasius would be returning to his see. This meeting ended, but the Arians sought other opportunities. Their last encounter with the Emperor was on the porch of the palace. Lucius himself asked Jovian, "May it please your Might, listen to me." Exasperated, the Emperor said,

"How did you come here, by sea or by land?" Lucius responded, "May it please you, by sea." Whereupon Jovian exclaimed, "Well, Lucius, may the God of the world, and the radiant sun, and moon, be angry with those men that made the voyage with you, for not casting you into the sea; and may that ship never again have fair winds, nor find a haven with her passengers in a storm."[55]

Following his meeting with Jovian, Athanasius left Antioch and arrived back in Alexandria in February of 364. Not long after this the new Emperor died from the fumes of a charcoal fire at a wayside inn. Valentinian was elected by the army to take his place. Valentinian then chose his brother Valens to rule in the East.

Athanasius remained at his see in peace about a year, when trouble struck again. An edict was published at Alexandria ordering the Patriarch to be expelled. Under penalty of heavy fines the civil authorities were told to expel all bishops who had been exiled by Constantius (even though they had been recalled by Julian). The authorities wanted to escape the fines. The people protested the order vehemently. In fact, riots began in the streets. The riots continued for a month. The prefect then quieted the people by assuring them that the matter had been referred to the Emperor.

The answer from the Emperor came in October. It was not diplomatic. Armed forces broke into the Church of Dionysius at night. The rooms of the clergy were searched in the attempt to arrest Athanasius. But he was gone. Warned ahead of time, he had escaped to his country house near the New River (an outlet branch of the Nile). This exile, however, was to be the shortest he had to endure. In autumn a dangerous revolt by Procopius brought panic into the eastern part of the Empire. This was no time to have Egypt in turmoil. The government now decided that it was more convenient for them to let the Church have their beloved Bishop back. Therefore, in February of 366 the notary

Brasidas publicly announced the recall of the Patriarch by imperial order. This time Athanasius did not have to seek out the authorities. They came to him. The notary and other officials went out in person to escort the Bishop back to Alexandria.

When Athanasius returned he was in the thirty-seventh year of his episcopate. Nearly half of that time he had been in exile. But he was not to be forced out again. He was to spend the last seven years of his life in Alexandria. Not all of it would be in peace, however. He had only been back in the city five months when a heathen mob burned the Church of the Caesareum. This time the authorities were on the side of justice. The arsonists were arrested and punished. The following year the Arians continued their efforts to replace the Patriarch. They met at Antioch and consecrated Lucius as a bishop. Though Jovian had rejected him, they sent Lucius to Alexandria anyway. In September of 367 he quietly entered the city at night. It was not long, however, before the public got wind of his arrival. His reception was not cordial. Soldiers had to rescue Lucius from the enraged populace. He was then escorted out of Egypt.

In his Paschal Letter for that same year Athanasius became the first Father of the early Church to put into writing a list of the canonical books of the Bible. He was concerned that some people might be led astray by reading apocryphal books. He expressed his concern, by saying: "I have been urged by genuine brothers and sisters, and instructed from the beginning, to set forth in order the canonized and transmitted writings, those believed to be divine books, so that those who have been deceived might condemn the persons who led them astray, and those who have remained pure might rejoice to be reminded.... These are the springs of salvation, so that someone who thirsts may be satisfied by the words they contain. In these books alone the teaching of

piety is proclaimed. Let no one add to or subtract from them."[56]
The whole Bible was dear to Athanasius. To him all the
books of Scripture were inspired by God and useful for instruction. But he was especially devoted to the Psalms. He viewed them
as a special treasure. "In the Psalter... you learn about yourself.
You find depicted in it all the movements of the soul, all its
changes, its ups and downs, its failures and recoveries." Throughout all the circumstances of life, the Psalms meet our own soul's
need at every turn. "Anyone who hears them is moved at heart, as
though they voiced for him his deepest thoughts.... The reader
takes all its words upon his lips as though they were his own, and
each one sings the Psalms as though they had been written for
his special benefit.... For I think that in the words of this book
all human life is covered, with all its states and thoughts."[57]
Athanasius had an encyclopedic knowledge of the Psalms. Like
many monks of his day, he undoubtedly had the entire Psalter
memorized.

In April of 368 the blessed monk Theodore passed away.
When the Patriarch learned of it he sent a letter of consolation to
Abba Horsiesios and the monks. The letter revealed his insight
into death and grieving: "Let us not weep over one who has gone
to that place from which weeping, mourning, and groaning have
fled, who is resting with his fathers.... Let us not grieve over one
who has tied up his boat in that fair haven which offers full secu-
rity, complete relief and all joy. Would that each of us might ex-
ert himself until he brings his boat into that haven. For, indeed,
Theodore is not dead but asleep in a good repose in the presence
of the Lord."[58]

The Bishop's last years were active ones. In May of 368 he
began the rebuilding of the burned Church of the Caesareum. In
that year the faithful celebrated the Patriarch's fortieth year in the

episcopate. In commemoration of this event the construction of a new church was begun in the Mendidium quarter of the city in September. In 369 he wrote his letter *To the Bishops of Africa*, giving an account of the Council of Nicea. In August of 370 the church in Mendidium was completed. It was dedicated in his honor.

The Patriarch lived long enough to witness the decline of Arianism (though factions of it continued on after his lifetime). The high point of the Arian cause had been during the reign of Constantius. With his death in 361, the Arians lost their most powerful supporter. In the years that followed, the heresy began to lose momentum. Key figures died. Others recanted and returned to the Church. The last Emperor to embrace Arianism was Valens, who died in 378. After the Second Ecumenical Council in 381, the Arian movement further declined to the point that it was no longer a major threat to the Church.

Athanasius' many years of service gave him the discernment of how to deal with many different kinds of situations. He was like a good physician who knew what medicine to apply and when. He knew when to be stern and when to be gracious. He was not afraid to use that discernment, either. It did not matter who was involved. The governor of Libya was an example of this. He was involved in a lifestyle of immoral behavior and was unwilling to repent. The Patriarch excommunicated him and made his decision known to the public. In other circumstances, however, Athanasius knew when to be gracious. At times he was willing to overlook the letter of the law in favor of mercy. In the diocese of Erythrum in Libya the inhabitants of two large villages clamored for a bishop of their own. Without the Patriarch's knowledge Bishop Philo consecrated as bishop a young army officer, named Siderius, who was there on civil duty. He did so without having two other bishops at the service with him as was canonically required. Athanasius overlooked this irregularity. He apparently understood the need for the appointment and the worthiness of the appointee. To him, showing mercy was sometimes better than following the letter of the law. Indeed, the Patriarch even later elevated Siderius to the Metropolitan see of Ptolemais.

In his last years Athanasius began correspondence with Basil of Caesarea. Basil had been consecrated bishop of that region in 370. The two shared a mutual respect for each other. Both were champions of Nicene Christology. Frequent letters passed between the two, but only those of Basil are extant. In one letter Basil wrote to Athanasius: "The more the disorders of the Church increase, the more do we turn toward [you]…, believing that the one consolation left to us in our dangers lies in your leadership. You, indeed, have saved us from this terrible storm by the power of your prayers and by your knowledge of how to give the best suggestions in our troubles…. Therefore, do not be remiss in praying for us and encouraging us by your letters."[59]

As Athanasius neared the end of his life, his thoughts were not about this earth. In his last Paschal Letter he was looking forward to the citizenship of Heaven: "Whereas, we were strangers, we are called friends. From being formerly aliens, we have become fellow-citizens with the saints, and are called children of the Jerusalem which is above…. Let us… enter into the holy place, …where also our Forerunner Jesus is entered for us, having obtained eternal redemption."[60]

In the seventy-fifth year of his life and in the forty-sixth year of his episcopate, Athanasius realized that the end of his days was drawing near. Following the example of his predecessor, the much revered Alexander, he recommended a successor to follow him. The one whom he deemed most worthy to succeed him as bishop was a faithful man named Peter. Then on the night of May 2, 373 the blessed Patriarch departed this life in peace. The wonderful Bishop, who had battled for so long and so hard as the champion of truth, now entered into eternal glory. He had been exiled one last time — from Earth to Heaven.

ALEXANDRIA

Saint Athanasius lived in Alexandria, on the coast of the Mediterranean Sea. The capital of Egypt, it was one of the great cities of the ancient world. It was a hub of trade, a center for scholarship, and a crossroads of cultures. Alexandria in the three centuries before Christ was the greatest city in the civilized world. In Athanasius' day it had been eclipsed only by Rome. Despite this, it still remained the world's center for academic learning and scientific research.

Alexandria was founded by the great military leader Alexander the Great and the city bears his name. In a span of a few years this conqueror from Macedonia established a kingdom which stretched from Greece in the north, to Egypt in the south, to India in the East. During his military campaign against the Persian Empire he took control of Egypt, which for centuries had been under Persian rule. He was greeted as a deliverer, since the Egyptians hated the Persians. It was in that year (332 B.C.) that Alexander ordered the founding of a new city, which in time would become the capital city of Egypt.

Alexander chose a site for the city after consulting with experts in navigation, trade, and architecture. The city was to be built on the shore of the Mediterranean Sea near the village of Rhakotis.

Buffered from storms by the nearby island of Pharos, it had an ideal harbor. The site lay on a ridge which separated the sea from the nearby freshwater Lake Mareotis. It was near the Canopic mouth of the Nile River. The climate was temperate due to prevailing winds off the sea. Designed by the architect Deinokratis of Rhodes, the city was laid out in a grid pattern with a great east-west thoroughfare (100 feet wide). It had two principal gates: the eastern Gate of the Sun and the western Gate of the Moon. Alexander commissioned his finance minister, Cleomenes of Naudratis, to supervise and finance the construction of the city. Then Alexander continued on with his military campaigns. He never saw the city built. He died eight years later (ironically, from a fever and not from battle). His body was later entombed in the grand city which he had envisioned.

After Alexander's death his empire was divided among his generals, who later proclaimed themselves as independent kings. The general Ptolemy took control of Egypt. It was under his reign, and that of his successors, the Ptolemies, that Alexandria grew to become one of the greatest and most influential cities on earth. It remained so for a thousand years, first under the Ptolemies, then under the Romans, and, finally, within the Byzantine Empire.

The building of the city continued over a long period of time. A causeway, called the Heptastadion was built to the island Pharos, thus forming a double harbor. Beside the Great Harbor, an enormous lighthouse was built. Considered one of the seven wonders of the ancient world, it was 350 feet high. Its powerful light, fueled by burning wood and magnified by convex mirrors, could be seen fifty miles out at sea. To aid navigation a canal was dug connecting Lake Mareotis with the Nile River. The city continued to grow as buildings of all kinds were constructed: fortifications, palaces, temples, schools, libraries, theaters, and tombs. Among these were: the Gymnasium, a high school/university; the Palaestra, akin to the modern concept of a gymnasium; and the Dicasterion (the Palace of Justice). Numerous temples were built to various Greek, Egyptian, and later Roman gods. Under Soter's reign a new god was even invented for the city. "Serapis" was an amalgamation of Greek and Egyptian deities. A huge temple called the Serapeum was built in his honor. Later under Roman rule an eighty-foot high column was erected. It was commonly referred to as Pompey's Pillar, despite the fact that it had been built in honor of Emperor Diocletian. The public buildings were faced with marble, which gave the city a gleaming-white appearance. The two main streets were the Canopic Way, which was bordered by colonnades its entire length, and the Street of the Soma, which had an avenue of trees down the middle. Both were lighted at night by oil lamps. The city was well supplied with water and there were several fountains in the Palace gardens.

Over time the population of the city grew to over 300,000 people (not counting slaves). The city was divided into five quarters. One area was Jewish, another Egyptian, and the rest were primarily Greek. However, the city was also home to many others, including Libyans, Cilicians, Ethiopians, Arabs, Bactrians, Scythians, and Indians.

So majestic was the city that even centuries after its zenith the Arab conqueror, Amr Ibn el As, wrote in 642 A.D., "I have taken a city which I can but say contains 4,000 palaces, 4,000 baths, 400 cellars, 1,200 sellers of green vegetables."[61]

Alexandria was one of the greatest sea ports in the ancient world. Exports and imports flowed through the city in vast quantities. In the second century, Dio of Prusa addressed the Alexandrians, by saying: "Not only have you a monopoly of the shipping of the entire Mediterranean because of the beauty of your harbors, the magnitude of your fleet, and the abundance and marketing of the products of every land, but also the outer waters that lie beyond are in your grasp, both the Red Sea and the Indian Ocean.... The result is that the trade, not merely of islands, ports, a few straits and isthmuses, but of practically the whole world is yours."[62]

Under the reign of the Ptolemies agriculture was improved in the surrounding region. A vast irrigation system was built. Swamp land was drained, and desert reclaimed. Vineyards were improved and the cultivation of olives and garlic was introduced. Pigs were imported, along with new breeds of sheep. Horses and even war elephants were brought in for the army. More importantly, new strains of wheat were introduced, which increased crop production. In time this led to the major export of grain. Much of it was sent to Rome, first as trade but later as tribute. Mines and quarries were also developed. Iron was brought from the eastern desert, gold from Nubia, and granite from Aswan.

Alexandria became the center of many industries, including textiles, papyrus paper (of which it had a monopoly), glass, oil, perfumes, wine, as well as ivory and ebony work. Goods arrived from Africa, Arabia, Greece, Rome, and even India. (The discovery of the seasonal winds in the Arabian Sea, westerly in summer and easterly in winter, made for a quicker trade route to India.) So great was the trade and commerce of the city that it was nicknamed the "Mistress of the Sea."

In the reign of Philadelphus even a zoo was established. It contained lions, leopards, cape buffaloes, wild donkeys, a giant python, a giraffe, a rhinoceros, a polar bear, as well as parrots, peacocks, and other birds.

The prosperity of Egypt attracted many Greek immigrants. Their growing numbers soon formed a sizable Greek community and they became the ruling class, enjoying special privileges. The impact of Greek culture was such that Alexandria, essentially, became a "Greek city" within an Egyptian nation. Greek became the official language of government. (In fact, Cleopatra VII was the only Ptolemaic ruler ever even to learn the Egyptian language.) The citizens of Alexandria had somewhat of a reputation. Others derided them for their hotheadedness, misconduct, passionate contentions, and pursuit of pleasure. Resentment for Roman rule was also strong. The philosopher Seneca remarked that the Egyptians had a positive genius for deriding their Roman governors. Undoubtedly, the citizens of Alexandria led the way.

One of the greatest achievements of the Alexandrians was the Great Library, and its research center, the Museum. Founded by Ptolemy I in 295 B.C., these twin institutions were financed and maintained with royal funds. Demetrius of Phaleron was appointed to be the first head of the library and he was commissioned "to collect all the books in the world." Within fifty years so many books had been collected that a second library had to be built to contain them. The number of manuscripts collected was nearly 500,000 (in papyrus scrolls). It was the greatest library in the ancient world.

The Museum was patterned after the philosophical schools of Athens. Its name was derived from the "Muses" (in Greek mythology the nine daughters of the god Zeus). The Museum rapidly gained international fame and attracted the best minds of the age. The foremost scholars of every branch of knowledge gathered there. The advantages provided to these scholars included: free room and board, financial support, and even exemption from taxes. Though the scholars had a certain degree of autonomy, their status depended largely on the whim of the government. They led a rather cloistered life, and took little part in public affairs. The

Museum was founded as a research center and, so in the beginning, it had no regular teaching, though eminent members did have pupils and assistants. Over time the role of teaching became more predominant. During the Roman era, the Museum offered the best academic training available anywhere.

The fields of study at the Museum included: literature, mathematics, physics, medicine, geography, and astronomy. A number of those associated with the Museum acquired international fame. Callimachus was one of its most famous poets. Euclid is considered the father of mathematics. Erastosthenes calculated the diameter of the earth (to within fifty actual miles). Aristarchus observed that the sun, and not the earth, was the center of the solar system. In medicine Herophilus advanced the understanding of the circulatory and nervous systems. The engineer Hero devised simple steam engines (though they were not put to practical use). Claudius Ptolemaeus' work was considered the last word in geography up until the Renaissance. It was at the Museum that our modern calendar was formulated. Two of the most prominent Alexandrian philosophers were Philo and Plotinus. It was also in Alexandria around the year 200 B.C. that Jewish scholars translated the Old Testament into the Greek language. This translation, called the Septuagint (named after the seventy translators), remains as one of the most important translations in history.

Diplomatic relations with Rome were initiated by Ptolemy II in 273 B.C. In time Rome began to provide protection for Egypt against its enemies. During the two centuries that followed, the influence of Rome over Egypt steadily increased. Correspondingly, the power of the Ptolemaic rulers diminished. With the invasion of Julius Caesar in 47 B.C. the reign of the Ptolemies was nearing its end. It ended altogether with the death of Cleopatra thirteen years later. Outright Roman rule began under Augustus

Caesar. With Roman rule, Alexandria lost its Senate and with it self-government. Local councils were not allowed again for more than two hundred years.

Though Alexandrian society had upper and middle classes, most Egyptians were poor. The prolonged prosperity of the city attracted many people from the countryside. During seasons when the annual Nile flood failed to irrigate the fields as needed, many peasants abandoned their villages for the city, hoping to find employment. The end result was overcrowding in the Egyptian quarter.

In the third century, civil war and an outbreak of the plague weakened the city. The establishment of Constantinople as the new imperial city in the fourth century further undermined Alexandria's status in the East. Later under Arab domination in the seventh century Cairo supplanted it as the capital city of Egypt. With it the golden age of Alexandria ended.

LIFE IN EGYPT

Life in Egypt centered around the great Nile River. Flowing four thousand miles from the East African highlands to the Mediterranean Sea, it is the longest river in the world. Its annual floodwaters irrigated lowland areas and left behind rich alluvial soil. This alluvial soil was called "a gift of the river" by Herodotus the Greek historian. Indeed, without this gift the lower Nile Valley would have been a desert.

The Nile in Egypt had two distinct areas: the Valley and the Delta. In ancient times, the Valley was referred to as Upper Egypt and the Delta as Lower Egypt. (Each of these areas was divided into provinces called nomes. Upper Egypt had twenty-two nomes and Lower Egypt had twenty.) The Valley was over six hundred miles long and six to twelve miles wide. The Delta region was an area formed by the seven branches of the Nile River that emptied into the Mediterranean. The Greeks named it the "Delta" because of its triangular shape, which reminded them of the fourth letter of the Greek alphabet. Each side of its triangular shape was about one hundred and twenty miles in length.

Each year the Nile would rise to flood stage in July and begin to recede in September. From ancient times the Egyptians had observed a direct relationship between the height of the floodwaters and the bounty of their crops. To predict this relationship with precision, "nilometers" (either natural or man-made stone structures) were used to measure the height of the waters. From these readings the size of the crop harvests could be predicted, and the government could estimate its tax revenues as well. In years when the floodwaters were too low, or too high, hardship or even famine could ensue. Pliny the Elder wrote, "Egypt reckons as follows: with 12 cubits [on the nilometer] it faces famine, at 13 it is still hungry, 14 cubits brings happiness, 15 freedom from worry, 16 delight."[63]

An extensive irrigation-system of dikes, canals, and basins was used to direct and store the flood waters. Considerable maintenance was required to maintain this irrigation system and prevent it from silting up. This was accomplished through the practice of conscripted labor. Every able-bodied male peasant was required to perform five (unpaid) days of labor each year.

The Nile was one of the great trading routes of the ancient world. Boats ranging from one-man skiffs to thirty-foot vessels plied its waters. Both oars and sails were used for upstream travel. Night travel was avoided because of the danger of running aground on sandbars or islands. The depth of the water greatly affected the speed of travel. At flood season a voyage from Thebes to Memphis (about 550 miles) would take two weeks. At low water it could take two months. By far the largest shipments on the Nile were those of grain sent to Alexandria.

The structure of society within Egypt was much like that of the great pyramids. At the top were the official citizens of Rome. Below them were the Greeks of the urban areas. At the bottom were the great masses of people which the Romans disdainfully called "the Egyptians." These were the merchants, artisans, small landowners, townspeople, and peasants of the villages. (Slaves were outside of this social pyramid altogether. They were employed mostly in domestic work and not in agriculture, since they could not be used any cheaper than the vast number of peasants who farmed at a bare subsistence level.) The population overall was concentrated in a few large cities and in a large number of small villages. Most Egyptians were farmers. The poorest of these were tenant farmers. They lived in villages or hamlets and owned no farm land, just a small residence, a few tools, a few animals, a few sticks of furniture. They traveled daily to work in the fields, which could be a considerable distance from their homes.

A typical household was often an extended family, consisting of grandparents, parents, and grandchildren. Family size might range anywhere from two to twenty-two. Seven or eight was about average. If poor, a dozen or more family members might live together in a single small room. Birth rates were high but so was the rate of infant mortality. Life expectancy (with infant mortality factored in) was only twenty-five to thirty years. Of those who survived to age fifteen only half would live to age twenty-five, and only half of these would live to age thirty-five. This accounted for many widowed households, second marriages, and stepchildren. Most young men were married by age eighteen. Women were usually already mothers by the age of fifteen or sixteen.

Schooling usually began at about the age of ten. Boys and, occasionally, girls were taught in schools that were essentially private. Most teachers were men, but some were women. (Some slaves also served as teachers.) Studies included grammar, arithmetic, rhetoric, and the Greek classics. Any schooling beyond the basic level would require a stay in Alexandria. Primary education was not restricted to the Greek class. For example, a slave might be apprenticed to learn writing. Trade skills were learned through a period of apprenticeship. Yet for most of the poor an education would simply consist of learning how to survive by farming.

Greek was the predominant written language, although the native Egyptian language was also written in Coptic, an adaptation of the Greek alphabet. (Latin was used only a little.) Though Hellenism increased the level of literacy within the country, there were still many who could not read or write. To serve them, scribes "set up shop" in the streets. There sitting cross-legged with a tablet in their laps, they wrote letters, devised documents, and drew up contracts. The business of the poor was conducted in the street.

Clothing consisted of tunics of linen or wool. Bright colors were popular, with green, red, and blue being the favorites.

Most villagers ate what they grew. Wheat was the staple crop, used for making bread. Barley was grown for making beer (which was as much a food as a drink). Common vegetables were lettuce, cucumbers, leeks, onions, beans, peas, and radishes. Fruits harvested were melons, dates, figs, and pomegranates. Olive oil was used not only in cooking but also for health purposes and as fuel for lamps. Grapes were used to make wine. A variety of herbs were grown for medicinal purposes. Wild berries were gathered. Marshlands provided the all-useful papyrus plant. From it came paper, food, fuel, and all kinds of woven products. Sheep and goats provided meat, milk, and cheese (for those who could afford to own them or to buy their products). Fish were plentiful. They were eaten fresh, pickled, or dried. Waterfowl were abundant during the inundation. They were trapped with nets or snares.

The nun Egeria, who traveled through Lower Egypt and the Nile Valley in the late fourth century, recorded in her diary: "We traveled through the whole land of Gessem [about 160 miles south of Alexandria], constantly passing among vineyards which produce wine and other fields which produce balsam, past orchards, heavily cultivated fields, and numerous gardens, along the banks of the river Nile.... What can I add? I do not think that I have ever seen a more beautiful land."[64]

Both public and private lands were often leased out to others for farming. Sometimes middlemen would sublease these lands. When the poor could not afford to buy seed for planting, they would have to borrow it. The seed was paid back at harvest time (plus interest). A vicious circle was sometimes the result: borrowing, planting, harvesting, and borrowing again. A barter economy was standard in the countryside. (In the cities banks were used for large transactions.) Hired hands were often paid in food: two loaves of bread per day.

Trade workers were organized into guilds (more for the government's benefit than for their own). Some of the trades included: builders, stone cutters, brick makers, brick layers, carpenters, potters, metal workers, bakers, butchers, barbers, shoe makers, dyers, fullers, embroiderers, and weavers. Women were commonly employed as wet nurses. Actors and athletes had their own organizations as well. The best of them developed large followings and received special privileges, such as tax exemption.

Taxes were ubiquitous. There were poll taxes, farm taxes, animal taxes, land taxes, dike taxes, handicraft taxes, occupational taxes, property taxes, military taxes, plus tolls and tariffs. A census was periodically taken, the underlying purpose being to aid tax collection. Soldiers could also "assist" in tax collection. Besides outright taxes there were also "liturgies" to perform. These were periodic, unpaid, public duties assigned to the general populace. When the burden of all these became too great, some people simply ran away. Often they ended up in Alexandria, where they could melt into the population and hope to find employment.

The predominant buildings in the cities were the record

office, civic treasury, council chamber, theater, the gymnasium, the public baths, and sometimes a hippodrome. The gymnasium was the central focus for the Greeks of the town. It contained lecture halls and classrooms, ball courts, a gym in the modern sense, and baths. Public baths met a common and real need, since domestic water was only available to the wealthy or large institutions. Some baths had separate areas for men and women. Others did not.

Though timber for building was scarce (most of it had to be imported), minerals were plentiful. Aswan granite was used in monuments up and down the river. The eastern desert contained copper, iron, and lead. Gold mines lay to the south. (Criminals and slaves were used to work the mines.)

Houses were often built end to end in rows, with narrow streets between the rows. They were made of sun-dried bricks, which lasted almost indefinitely in the dry, desert climate. The outer walls were thick, made of several courses of bricks. Windows were few, since the Egyptians welcomed a respite from the sun. Two story houses were common. They consisted of one to three rooms, which housed animals as well as the family. Homes of the more well-to-do had underground rooms with vaulted arches, a ground floor, a second, and, sometimes, a third floor. Most houses had courtyards around which much activity revolved. They contained animal pens, millstones for grinding wheat, and clay ovens for baking bread. Most people lived in their village from the cradle to the grave.

Public entertainment included such things as chariot races, gymnastic shows, athletic events, and artistic performances. Traveling guilds brought dramatic or musical presentations. The flute was a favorite instrument and Alexandria was renowned for its flute-players. On a more modest level there were mimes, poetic recitations, singing, dancing, amateur chariot races, jugglers, and acrobats.

Most medicine simply consisted of home remedies, passed down from one generation to the next. (Physicians were available in the cities.) The wide use of river water led to the spread of disease, especially during the periods of inundation. Diseases of the eye and foot were particularly common.

The religions of three cultures came together in Egypt. There were temples to Egyptian, Greek, and Roman gods. These various faiths not only co-existed, but often blended together. One of the most popular cults of Egypt was that of Isis, the life-giver, whose worship spread throughout the Mediterranean. The cult of Serapis was common to all major towns. His advice was sought through oracles and dreams. Hapi was the god of the river, Khnum the fashioner of mankind, Anuket the dispenser of cool water. Nile creatures like the hippopotamus, crocodile, and fish were venerated as gods of fertility. The river Nile itself was worshipped, as one prayer read: "Rule the streams, O Nile of many floods, of great name. From Meroe flow down to us, gracious and welcome."[65]

THE CHURCH IN EGYPT

Egypt was no stranger to God. In Old Testament times the patriarchs Abraham and Jacob both visited this ancient land. There Joseph was sold into slavery, only to gain his freedom and rise in power second only to Pharaoh. His family was to remain there. It grew both into a great nation and into slavery. There the prophet Moses was rescued by Pharaoh's daughter and with many signs and wonders led the nation of Israel out of captivity. In New Testament times Egypt became a refuge for the Holy Family. Fleeing the persecution of Herod, Joseph and Mary took the infant Jesus into hiding there until it was safe to return home.

According to tradition, Saint Mark the Evangelist brought Christianity to Alexandria in about 61 A.D. Annianos was ordained by him as the first bishop of the city. In time the office of bishop, like the status of the city, grew to great importance. The bishop became the patriarch over all Egypt. Egypt proved to be fertile ground for the spread of the gospel. The idea of resurrection was part of Egyptian pagan belief, and this aided the acceptance of Christianity. By the early third century the Church had twenty bishops serving different parts of the Nile region.

Alexandria was home to the famous School of Alexandria. It was the first center for Christian studies in the history of the

Church. Originally established as a catechetical school to prepare candidates for baptism, the role of the School expanded over time to include the teaching of the sciences, philosophy, and theology. Clement, one of the famous deans of the School at the end of the second century, mentions that the School in his day had three courses of study: a course for non-Christians, a course on Christian morals, and a course in advanced theology. Worship went hand in hand with study. Teachers and pupils alike participated in prayer, fasting, and asceticism. Many converts came to Christ through the teaching of the School. Out of the School also came many Church leaders and bishops. Its reputation also drew students from abroad. Some of its teachers traveled and taught outside of Egypt. One of the most distinctive teachings of the School was its allegorical interpretation of the Scriptures (in which the underlying meaning of a passage would be considered of great importance, often more so than the literal meaning).

Several of the School's deans were quite famous. Athengoras had been a philosopher at the Museum. In about 170 A.D. he converted to Christianity. He became an apologist for the faith and a dean of the school. Clement was both a priest and a dean of the School. The author of several books, he is considered to be the first systematic teacher of Christian doctrine. His pupil Origen was even more famous. Perhaps the most brilliant scholar of the early Church, Origen became head of the School of Alexandria while only eighteen years of age. He was a super-prolific writer. One of his many works was the Hexapla, a sixfold Old Testament in parallel columns from Hebrew and Greek texts. Unfortunately, in spite of his many achievements, some of Origen's ideas were heretical. A council later condemned his belief in the pre-existence of souls and the universal salvation of all.

Two great persecutions rocked the Church in Egypt in the

third century. Around 200 A.D. the Emperor Severus launched a persecution of Christians from Alexandria. Prisoners were brought from all over Egypt for trial and martyrdom. The School of Alexandria was a special target. To avoid arrest Clement and a group of teachers fled to Palestine. Origen, his successor as dean, wanted to be martyred. However, he was spared, while his father Leonides was killed. Fifty years later, a more systematic persecution swept through the Empire under the Emperor Decius. During this period Cyprian, the Bishop of Carthage, was martyred. Then peace returned to the Church for a period of forty years.

In the year 303 the great persecution under Diocletian began. It afflicted the Church throughout the Empire until 311, and continued in Egypt until 313. The persecution was so terrible that it is a wonder that the Church even survived. It is only by the grace of God that it did. All churches were closed. Many were desecrated, destroyed, or burned. Christianity was made illegal. The clergy were especially targeted by the officials. They were beaten, scourged, imprisoned, exiled, forced into hard labor, tortured, and killed. All Christians suffered in one way or the other. There were no public places left in which to worship and no clergy to lead the services. The terror mercifully came to an end with the conversion of Emperor Constantine the Great and his legalization of Christianity.

During the persecution a schismatic group began within the Church of Egypt. It began over the question of how to deal with those who had lapsed from the faith. Bishop Peter of Alexandria took a merciful approach and established a set of guidelines for receiving the lapsed. Bishop Melitius of Lycopolis, however, opposed him and wanted to deal harshly with the lapsed. Those who followed him were called the Meletians. The rift was widened when Meletius started to ordain clergy outside of his own diocese, contrary to Church canons. The Meletians were zealots who considered themselves to be the "pure Christians." However, they later showed their true colors when they united themselves with the Arian heretics. Their group continued on for several decades and they were a problem with which Athanasius had to deal throughout his episcopacy.

There was tremendous growth in the Church during this time. In the early part of the fourth century under Constantine's reign, it has been estimated that nearly half of all Egyptians were Christians. By the end of the century Egypt was, perhaps, the most Christian place on earth. Christians made up an estimated 80-90% of the population. In Athanasius' day there were several churches within the city of Alexandria alone. Some of these included the churches of: Saint John the Baptist, Saints Cosmas and Damian, Saint Peter, Saint Mark the Evangelist, and Saint Mary Dorothea.

CONSTANTINE

Of all the great figures of the fourth century Constantine stands near the top. He unified the Roman Empire under his sole leadership and brought many reforms to the government. Of all his deeds during three decades of leadership he will be eternally remembered for his aid to the Church. Indeed, he has been canonized a saint for just that.

Constantine was the son of Constantius and Helen. His father Constantius was an officer in the imperial army, who rose all the way to the rank of Caesar. To further his career, he had divorced his wife Helen and married the daughter of Emperor Diocletian. As Caesar he ruled over the regions of Gaul and Britain. It is possible that Constantius was a "closet Christian." His behavior toward Christians would seem to indicate so. In the West he had kept the persecution to a minimum. Also, one of his daughters bore the Christian name of Anastasia.

Constantine's mother Helen was also canonized like her son. At what point she became a Christian is uncertain. But later in life she was a prominent figure in the Church. Her pilgrimages to the Holy Land are well-known. On one of these she made the famous discovery of the Holy Cross. She also provided for the building of new churches in Jerusalem.

Constantine followed in his father's footsteps and entered the military. He became a successful and well-accepted officer. For a time he actually ended up in the court of the Emperor Diocletian. Later he joined his father in the West. There he distinguished himself in a military campaign against rebel forces in Britain. Upon the death of Constantius in the year 305, Constantine was proclaimed the new Caesar in his father's place. Like his father before him, he favored the Christians. Whether Constantine had been exposed to the Christian faith as a child is uncertain. Somewhere along the line, though, he gained at least an awareness of his destiny. For by the time of his military service in the West he could say, "God sought my services in Britain as His instrument for freeing the world."[66] At this point his understanding of Christianity may not have been clear. It became so at the Battle of the Milvian Bridge.

During this period the Empire had three Caesars: Constantine in the West, Maxentius in Rome, and Galerius in the East. Diocletian had been the one to devise this system. As a sole Emperor he had sought out co-Caesars to help him rule different regions of the vast Roman Empire. Then he retired with the hope that his system of shared power would improve and consolidate the Empire. It had the opposite effect. Infighting and jealousy was the result.

Thereafter, it became Constantine's goal to unify the Empire. He marched on Rome to unseat the pagan Maxentius. A string of victories in battle led him to the outskirts of Rome. The city was considered impregnable and Maxentius' forces seemed safe within the city walls. But then a strange turn of events occurred. It was to have a result of historic proportions. Maxentius looked for a sign. He had the pagan priests consult the Sibylline Books. They pronounced a prophecy that on the next day the enemy of Rome would perish. (It never occurred to Maxentius that he might be that enemy.) Assured by the prophecy, Maxentius now felt confident that he would defeat Constantine's army. But to defeat Constantine, there would have to be a battle, and for there to be a battle, Maxentius would have to go outside the city walls and fight.

That same day Constantine saw a vision. In the sky in broad daylight there appeared a pillar of light in the shape of a cross. On the cross were inscribed the words: "by this sign conquer." In a dream the following night Constantine was directed to prepare the labarum, a banner with the chi-rho (the first two Greek letters of the word Christ) monogram. His troops were also to trace these letters on their shields. Fighting under the labarum, he was told, his troops would be victorious. As a military man Constantine knew how to follow orders. He accepted the vision in the sky and his dream as the calling of God. (This event is often referred to as the conversion of Constantine to the Christian faith. This may be so. But it is also possible that Constantine already had a degree of faith which was solidified by these miraculous signs.)

Before dawn Maxentius' troops left the city and crossed the Tiber River at the Milvian Bridge to begin their attack. At first the element of surprise gave them the upper hand, but Constantine rallied his troops. A fierce battle ensued. Slowly the tide turned. Maxentius' forces were pushed back to the river. They panicked and attempted to flee back across the bridge. Trapped in a bottleneck at the bridge, they were soundly defeated. Maxentius himself was pushed off his horse into the river and drowned in his heavy armor. Constantine marched into Rome victorious. The year was 312.

Constantine now controlled Rome and the West. His ally Licinius took control of the East (Galerius having died the year before). At first things went well between the two, but then a change came over Licinius. It was, perhaps, madness. He descended into debauchery and cruelty. Previously, he had at least seemed neutral toward Christianity, but now he began to persecute the Church. The inevitable occurred. Constantine and Licinius met each other in battle. In the year 323 Licinius was defeated. Constantine became the sole ruler of the Roman Empire.

More importantly, Constantine was the first Christian Emperor. The impact of this upon the Church and the civilization of mankind was profound. Under his reign the great persecution came to an end. Christianity was no longer an illegal and persecuted religion. In fact, under Constantine it became the favored religion of the Empire. Prisoners were freed. Exiles were returned. Confiscated property was restored. Justice was given to those who had suffered during the persecution. Public funds were used to rebuild the churches. Clergy were given exemption from taxes and compulsory public service. Sunday was made a public holiday. The celebration of pagan festivals was prohibited. Constantine built Constantinople, the new imperial city of the East. It was graced with many churches and cathedrals. When the Arian heresy began to rend the Church, Constantine called the First Ecumenical Council to deal with it. Bishops and leaders of the Church were brought to Nicea and supported there at government expense. Indeed, it would be difficult to catalog the many ways in which Constantine aided the Church and mankind in general.

Though Constantine could proclaim: "I owe my life and breath, my inmost secret thoughts to God,"[67] he was by no means perfect. Some of his dealings with his own family and with Saint Athanasius and others point this out. But his overall contribution to the Church was immense. He reversed three long centuries of intolerance from the imperial throne and replaced it with the blessing of peace. His imperial reign had more impact upon Christianity than that of any other ruler who ever lived. Because of this he is honored by the Church with the title: "equal to the apostles."

MONASTICISM

Monasticism has its roots in the Old Testament. Several of the prophets of Israel were precursors to the ascetic life. They dwelt in deserted places, lived meagerly, and sought after God. The most famous of these prophets was John the Baptist. He lived in the desert, wore a hair shirt, and ate locusts and honey. Though removed from people, he was, nonetheless, close to God.

From the very beginnings of the Church there were those who voluntarily chose to live a celibate life. In Alexandria these included both men and women. They came from every level of society. The men were called "solitaries" and the women were called "virgins." (The terms "monk" and "nun" came later.) They devoted themselves to fasting, prayer, and vigil. They lived in the city and worshipped in the parish church. Men lived alone or in small groups. Women usually lived either with their parents or with other virgins.

Monasticism as an institution began to take shape early in the fourth century. Solitaries started to retreat from the city and to dwell apart in the desert. The most famous of these hermits was Antony. About 313 Antony crossed the Nile and journeyed into the desert. There he shut himself up in a deserted fort. In solitude he devoted himself to prayer, fasting, and vigil. Bread was brought to him twice a year. He provided for himself by weaving.

(The making of baskets, mats, rope, and sandals from palm-blades and rushes became the main industry for monks. This simple, monotonous work was conducive to the practice of unceasing prayer.)

Antony remained in solitude and was rarely seen by anyone. He endured intense attacks from the demons. Through great asceticism Antony was purified of evil passions and led into divine mysteries. He spent twenty years in solitude. As his spiritual feats became known, others desired to emulate him. In time so many took up the solitary life after his example, that Athanasius, his biographer, remarked that the "desert was made a city by monks, who left their own people and registered themselves for the citizenship in the heavens."[68] Those who lived this kind of solitary existence were called eremites or anchorites.

About 330 Ammoun founded a loosely connected series of monastic retreats in the Nitrian desert. Before entering the desert, he and his wife had lived together for eighteen years as brother and sister. Ammoun's monastic community was the first to have its own clergy. These monastics lived a less solitary life than the anchorites. Small groups of them lived together in "sketes" or "lavras" under the direction of a spiritual father or "abba." Macarius was also one of the founders of this kind of monasticism, known as semi-eremitical.

Another form of monasticism, however, was to become the norm. It was called cenobitic, or communal monasticism. This ascetic way of life was centered around a monastery. Here larger groups of monks lived together in community life under the direction of an abbot. Their way of life was structured by a set, monastic rule. Pachomius was the first to found this form of monasticism. By the year 330 he had already begun to form a network of monasteries in the Thebaid along the Nile. He also founded a women's monastery near Tabennesi. In Pachomius' time the number of monks grew into the thousands.

Over time the layout of monasteries took on a pattern. The buildings were simple and made of sun-dried bricks. (Stone buildings came later.) The perimeter of the monastery was enclosed by a wall. The buildings of a large monastery included: a gate house, a guest house, an assembly hall for worship, a kitchen (and separate bake house), a refectory (dining hall), and a number of houses containing cells for each monk. There were also shops for maintenance work and other buildings for special trades. Agriculture was carried on outside the walls.

Life in the monastery was structured. A common meal was shared about midday. The monks retired early to sleep and arose about midnight. Their worship would continue until near dawn. Each individual house also had set hours of prayer. In addition, each monk prayed, meditated, and studied in his own cell. Spiritual instruction was given several times a week.

In this era most of the women monastics lived in or near the city. Athanasius acted as their spiritual guide. He recommended to them a life of seclusion, which included prayer, vigils, fasting, Scripture reading, the singing of the Psalms, and moderation in clothing, food, sleep, and conversation. "Speak like a dove, which barely speaks in her heart," he advised. "Do not, like a raven, make a lot of noise and commotion."[69] Athanasius was a strong supporter of the monks and they of him. He met the great Antony in his youth and they remained lifelong friends. Throughout the many trials of his life the monks were among his strongest supporters. From time to time, as his episcopal duties allowed, he returned to visit them. He spent several years among the monks during his latter exiles.

Athanasius praised the celibate life. While he regarded marriage as honorable and in accordance with nature, he said that "virginity surpasses human nature, for it is the image of angelic purity."[70] He called monasticism a "holy and heavenly profession."

A GUIDE FOR THE USE OF THE PSALMS

(adapted from Athanasius' Letter to Marcellinus)

The Conditions of Life and the Psalms Recommended for Them

affliction, help for - Psalm 51
alone, when you feel alone God is with you - Psalm 63
angry, when God is angry with His people - Psalm 74
appearance, against those who glory in appearance - Psalm 58
approaching God, with thankfulness and understanding - Psalm 29

baptized, be thankful when people are - Psalm 32
betrayal, when friends betray you - Psalm 55
blasphemy, when people blaspheme God - Psalms 14, 53
blessed, to declare someone blessed - Psalms 1, 32, 42, 112, 119, 128
boasting, when men boast of evil - Psalm 52

chrismation - Psalm 27
church, when rebuilding a destroyed one - Psalm 96
citizen, the quality of a heavenly one - Psalm 15
comfort those in distress - Psalm 20
comfort your soul - Psalm 42
confession - Psalm 51
conspiracy, rebuke the conspiracy against Jesus - Psalm 2
cry unto God, in weakness or when under attack - Psalm 28

dedicate your home - Psalm 127
dedicate your soul - Psalm 30
deliverance from evil men - Psalm 140

deliverance from your enemies - Psalm 18
deliverance, thanksgiving for - Psalms 85, 116
displeasure, when you are under God's - Psalms 6, 38
downcast, when you are - Psalm 102

encouragement - Psalm 91
endurance, value of - Psalm 40
enemies, pray against - Psalms 17, 86, 88, 140
enemies, victory over - Psalm 9
enemies, when they surround you - Psalm 25
evil council, when you have escaped from it - Psalm 34
evil men, pay no heed to them - Psalm 37
evil men, when they wait to harm you - Psalm 59

faint-hearted, do not be - Psalm 27
faith, express it - Psalms 11, 12
faith, instruct others in - Psalm 100
fathers of Israel, God's kindness to - Psalms 44, 78, 89, 105-6, 114-115
fear, do not fear in persecution - Psalm 63
fear, do not fear your enemies - Psalms 64, 70-71

goodness of God - Psalm 105
grace of our Savior - Psalm 8
guided, when you are by God - Psalm 23

heathens, a reply to - Psalm 76
heretics, a reply to - Psalm 76
hope against enemies - Psalm 83
hope in God - Psalm 42
hypocrites, against - Psalm 58

judgment of God - Psalm 101
judgment, trust in God's - Psalms 26, 35, 43
justice of God - Psalm 101

lawless, when the lawless are zealous for evil - Psalm 36
longing for the House of God - Psalm 84

marvel at Creation - Psalms 19, 24
marvel at the Law - Psalms 19, 24
mercy, ask for - Psalm 67
mercy, remembering God's mercy in affliction - Psalm 77
mercy, tell of God's - Psalm 46

Moses, how he prayed - Psalm 90

obedience, instruct others in - Psalm 100
opposed, when you are opposed by many - Psalm 3

peace after war - Psalm 97
persecuted by your family - Psalm 3
persecuted, when you are - Psalms 54, 56-7, 142
plead to God when his servants are martyred - Psalm 79
plot, when there is a plot against you - Psalm 7
poor, encourage those who help them - Psalm 41
praise, lift up a thankful heart - Psalms 103-4
praise, sing praise to God - Psalm 65
praise to God, from those who have been persecuted - Psalms 54, 56, 142
prayer and supplication - Psalms 5, 141-143, 146
prayer, faith that God has heard it - Psalm 116
prayer, morning - Psalm 5
pressing forward, forgetting what lies behind - Psalms 120-134
pride, when the evil speak from pride - Psalm 12
psalms of praise - Psalms 105-6, 113, 117, 135, 146-150

redemption, contemplate the redemption of humanity - Psalm 8
reflect on God's goodness - Psalms 44, 78, 89, 105-6, 114-115
reflect on the ungratefulness of man - Psalms 44, 78, 89, 105-6, 114-115
repentance - Psalm 51

safety, when your safety is in question - Psalm 39
schism, compared to the Church - Psalm 87
sing to the Lord - Psalms 96, 98
slandered, when you are - Psalms 54, 56
songs, on a festival - Psalms 81, 95
song to sing with others - Psalm 33
strayed, when you have strayed in sin - Psalm 137

temptation, when you have overcome - Psalm 139
testify about God - Psalms 9, 71, 75, 92, 105-108, 111, 118, 126, 136, 138
thanks to God, at the end of affliction - Psalms 4, 75, 116
thanks to God, for deliverance from affliction - Psalm 46
thanksgiving, on Friday - Psalm 93
thanksgiving, on the Lord's Day - Psalm 24
thanksgiving, on Monday - Psalm 95
trouble, when it does not cease - Psalm 27

trust in God, when a powerful enemy arises - Psalm 144
trust in God's will - Psalm 62

wicked, when the wicked alarm you - Psalm 11
wicked, when the wicked are in prosperity and peace - Psalm 73
wicked, when the wicked lie in wait for you - Psalm 5

Collated material taken from the *Letter to Marcellinus*, an appendix to *On the Incarnation*, a nun of the C.S.M.V., trans. and ed., St. Vladimir's Seminary Orthodox Press, Crestwood, 1953. Used by permission.

THE IMPORTANCE OF CHANTING
THE PSALMS

(excerpted from Athanasius' Letter to Marcellinus)

But we must not omit to explain the reason why words of this kind should be not merely said, but rendered with melody and song. For there are actually some simple folk among us who, though they believe the words to be inspired, yet think the reason for singing them is just to make them more pleasing to the ear! This is by no means so. Holy Scripture is not designed to tickle the aesthetic palate, and it is rather for the soul's own profit that the Psalms are sung. This is chiefly so for two reasons. In the first place, it is fitting that the sacred writings should praise God in poetry as well as prose, because the freer, less restricted form of verse, in which the Psalms, together with the Canticles and Odes, are cast, ensures that by them men should express their love to God with all the strength and power they possess. And, secondly, the reason lies in the unifying effect which chanting the Psalms has upon the singer. For to sing the Psalms demands such concentration of a man's whole being on them that, in doing so, his usual disharmony of mind and corresponding bodily confusion is resolved.... When, therefore, the Psalms are chanted, it is not from any mere desire for sweet music but as the outward expression of the inward harmony obtaining in the soul, because such harmonious recitation is in itself the index of a peaceful and well-ordered heart.... For a soul rightly ordered by chanting the sacred words forgets its own afflictions and contemplates with joy the things of Christ alone.

From the *Letter to Marcellinus*, an appendix to *On the Incarnation*, a nun of the C.S.M.V., trans. and ed., St. Vladimir's Seminary Orthodox Press, Crestwood, 1953. Used by permission.

NOTES

Volumes of the second series of the *Nicene and Post-Nicene Fathers of the Christian Church*, ed. P. Schaff (Eerdmans Publishing Co., Grand Rapids, reprinted 1975) are abbreviated as NPNF. Unless otherwise noted, the works of Athanasius are taken from Vol. IV. The Ecclesiastical Histories of Socrates and Sozomen are taken from Vol. II; of Theodoret from Vol. III.

[1] Athanasius, *On the Incarnation* (St. Vladimir's Seminary Press, Crestwood, 1953), p. 45.

[2] *Defense of the Nicene Definition*, VI.27.

[3] *Ibid.*, VI.25.

[4] Theodoret, I.3.

[5] *Councils of Ariminum and Seleucia*, 17.

[6] *Deposition of Arius*, 1.

[7] Theodoret, I.4.

[8] NPNF Vol. IV, p. 308.

[9] *History of the Arians*, I.3.

[10] Socrates, I.7.

[11] *Against the Gentiles*, III.46.

[12] Socrates, I.8.

[13] Socrates, I.9.

[14] Sozomen, II.17.

[15] NPNF Vol. IV, p. xxxvii.

[16] *Paschal Letter I*.

[17] A. Veilleux, trans., *Pachomian Koinonia* (Cisterian Publications, Kalamazoo, 1981), Vol. I, pp. 51-52. "Apa" is a variant form of "Abba": spiritual father.

[18] *Ibid.*, pp. 117-118.

[19] *Defense Against the Arians*, V.59.

[20] *Paschal Letter IV*. (The hymn "We will sing…" is from the Vesperal Liturgy of Saint Basil for Holy Saturday.)

[21] *Defense Against the Arians*, V.62.

[22] Socrates, I.29.

[23] *Paschal Letter X.*

[24] *Personal Letter LIV.*

[25] *Ibid.*

[26] *Paschal Letter XI.*

[27] Vielleux, Vol. I, p. 378.

[28] *Defense Against the Arians*, II.20.

[29] *Paschal Letter XIV.*

[30] *Defense Against the Arians*, IV.52.

[31] Veilleux, Vol. I, p. 192.

[32] *Defense Against the Arians*, IV.57.

[33] *Paschal Letter XIX.*

[34] *Ibid.*

[35] *History of the Arians*, III.25.

[36] Veilleux, Vol. II, p. 71.

[37] Athanasius, *Fragments on the Moral Life*; in *Athanasius and the Politics of Asceticism*, D. Brakke (Clarendon Press, Oxford, 1995), p. 314.

[38] *Defense before Constantius*, 15.

[39] *Ibid.*, 30.

[40] *Ibid.*, 31.

[41] *To the Bishops of Egypt*, I.3,5,23.

[42] Athanasius, *Paschal Letter 29*, D. Brakke, p. 325 (Scriptural passage of Romans 11:2 is from the text of Athanasius).

[43] R. Meyer, trans., *Palladius: the Lausiac History* (Newman Press, Westminster, MD, 1965), 63:4.

[44] *Defense of His Flight*, 22.

[45] *Personal Letter LI* (2nd letter to Lucifer, bishop of Calaria in Sardinia).

[46] *Ibid.*

[47] *Councils of Ariminum and Seleucia*, 54.

[48] NPNF Vol. IV, p. lix.

[49] Sozomen, V. 15.

[50] Veilleux, Vol. I, p. 251.

[51] *Ibid.*, p. 253.

[52] *Ibid.* ("If I forget you, O Jerusalem" is from Psalm 137; a psalm of exile sung by Israel while in captivity in Babylon. Psalm 137 is customarily sung in the Orthodox Matins services of Great Lent.)

[53] Veilleux, Vol. II, pp. 103-104.

[53] *Letter LVI.*

Notes

55 Appendix to *Letter LVI*.

56 Athanasius, *Paschal Letter 39*, Brakke, pp. 329-330.

57 Athanasius, *Letter to Marcellinus*, Appendix in *On the Incarnation* (St. Vladimir's Seminary Press), pp. 103-106.

58 Veilleux, Vol. I, p. 265.

59 A. Way, trans., *The Fathers of the Church*, Vol. 13: Saint Basil Letters (Catholic University of America Press, Washington, DC, 1965), p. 185.

60 *Paschal Letter XLV.*

61 J. Marlowe, *The Golden Age of Alexandria* (V. Gollancz Ltd., London, 1971), p. 13.

62 A. Bowman, *Egypt after the Pharaohs* (University of California Press, Hong Kong, 1986), p. 218.

63 N. Lewis, *Life in Egypt under Roman Rule* (Clarendon Press, Oxford, 1983), p. 110.

64 G. Gingras, trans., *Egeria: Diary of a Pilgrim, Ancient Christian Writers*, No. 38 (Newman Press, New York, 1970), p. 64.

65 Lewis, *ibid.*, p. 95.

66 T. Elliott, *The Christianity of Constantine the Great* (University of Scranton Press, Bronx, 1996), p. 134.

67 *Ibid.*

68 Athanasius, *The Life of Antony*, trans. R. Gregg (Paulist Press, New York, 1980), p. 43.

69 Athanasius, *Second Letter to Virgins*, 14; D. Brakke, p. 297.

70 *First Letter to Virgins*, 19, D. Brakke, p. 280.

BIBLIOGRAPHY

Volumes of the second series of the *Nicene and Post-Nicene Fathers of the Christian Church*, edited by P. Schaff (Eerdmans Publishing Co., Grand Rapids, reprinted 1975) are abbreviated as NPNF.

Writings of Saint Athanasius

(The works of Athanasius are taken from NPNF Vol. IV unless otherwise noted.)

Against the Gentiles.

Circular Letter.

Councils of Ariminum and Seleucia.

Defense Against the Arians.

Defense Before Constantius.

Defense of His Flight.

Defense of the Nicene Definition.

Deposition of Arius.

First Letter to Virgins, in *Athanasius and the Politics of Asceticism,* D. Brakke (Clarendon Press, Oxford, 1995).

Four Discourses Against the Arians.

Fragments on the Moral Life, Brakke.

History of the Arians.

Letter to Marcellinus, an appendix to *On the Incarnation,* a nun of the C.S.M.V., trans. and ed. (St. Vladimir's Seminary Orthodox Press, Crestwood, 1953).

Life of Antony, in *Athanasius: the Life of Antony and the Letter to Marcellinus,* R. Gregg, trans. (Paulist Press, New York, 1980).

On the Incarnation (St. Vladimir's Press).
On the Opinion of Dionysius.
Paschal Letters.
Personal Letters.
Second Letter to Virgins, Brakke.
Synodal Letter to the People of Antioch.
To the Bishops of Africa.
To the Bishops of Egypt.

Ancient Sources

Basil the Great: Letters; A. Way, trans., *The Fathers of the Church*, Vol. 13: *Saint Basil Letters* (Catholic University of America Press, Washington, DC, 1965).

Egeria the nun: Diary; G. Gingras, trans., *Ancient Christian Writers*, No. 38: *Egeria: Diary of a Pilgrim* (Newman Press, New York, 1970).

Eusebius: Church History; R. Defarrari, trans., *The Fathers of the Church*, Vol. 29: *The Ecclesiastical History of Eusebius* (Catholic University of America Press, Washington, DC, 1965).

Gregory Nazianzen: orations; NPNF, Vol. VII: *Orations of Gregory Nazianzen.*

Pachomian History; A. Veilleux, trans., *Pachomian Koinonia*, 2 Vols. (Cistercian Publications, Kalamazoo, 1981).

Palladius: Church History; R. Meyer, trans., *Palladius: the Lausiac History* (Newman Press, Westminster, 1965).

Socrates: Church History; NPNF, Vol. II: *Ecclesiastical History of Socrates.*

Sozomen: Church History; NPNF, Vol. II: *Ecclesiastical History of Sozomen.*

Theodoret: Church History; NPNF, Vol. III: *Ecclesiastical History of Theodoret.*

Bibliography

Resources

Arnold, D., *The Early Episcopal Career of Athanasius of Alexandria* (University of Notre Dame Press, Notre Dame, IN 1991).

Bowman, A., *Egypt after the Pharaohs* (University of California Press, Hong Kong, 1986).

Brakke, D., *Athanasius and the Politics of Asceticism* (Clarendon Press, Oxford, 1995).

Chitty, D., *The Desert a City* (St. Vladimir's Seminary Press, New York, 1966).

Elliott, T., *The Christianity of Constantine the Great* (University of Scranton Press, Bronx, 1996).

Forster, E.M., *Alexandria: a History and a Guide* (Oxford University Press, New York, 1986).

Kouloulas, D., *The Life and Times of Constantine the Great* (Rutledge Books, Danbury, 1997).

Lewis, N., *Life in Egypt under Roman Rule* (Clarendon Press, Oxford, 1983).

Malaty, T., *The School of Alexandria*, 2 vols. (St. Mark's Coptic Orthodox Church, Jersey City, 1994).

Marlowe, J., *The Golden Age of Alexandria* (V. Gollancz Ltd., London, 1971).

Momigliano, A., ed., *The Conflict between Paganism and Christianity in the Fourth Century* (Clarendon Press, Oxford, 1963).

Newman, J., *The Arians of the Fourth Century* (Wipf & Stock Publishers, Eugene, 1996).

Pettersen, A., *Athanasius* (Morehouse Publishing, Harrisburg, 1995).

Schaff, P., *History of the Christian Church*, Vol. I (Eerdmans Publ., Grand Rapids, reprinted 1976).

Silverman, D., ed., *Ancient Egypt* (Oxford University Press, New York, 1997).

Steen, G., ed., *Alexandria: the Site and the City* (Warner Books, New York, 1991).

Wahba, M., *Honorable Marriage according to St. Athanasius* (Light and Life Publ., Minneapolis, 1996).

_____, *The Doctrine of Sanctification in St. Athanasius' Paschal Letters* (Coptic Orthodox Church of Rhode Island, Cranston, 1988).